SIR FRANK FRANCIS, K.C.B., Litt.D., M.A., F.S.A., F.L.A.
President.

THE LIBRARY ASSOCIATION

Founded 1877 : Incorporated by Royal Charter 1898

YEAR BOOK

1965

1965

LONDON

THE LIBRARY ASSOCIATION

Chaucer House, Malet Place, W.C.1

Telephone : Euston 5856 (4 lines) *Telegrams :* Euston 5856 London

Telex : 21897

PRINTED IN GREAT BRITAIN BY HEADLEY BROTHERS LTD
109 KINGSWAY LONDON WC2 AND ASHFORD KENT

CONTENTS

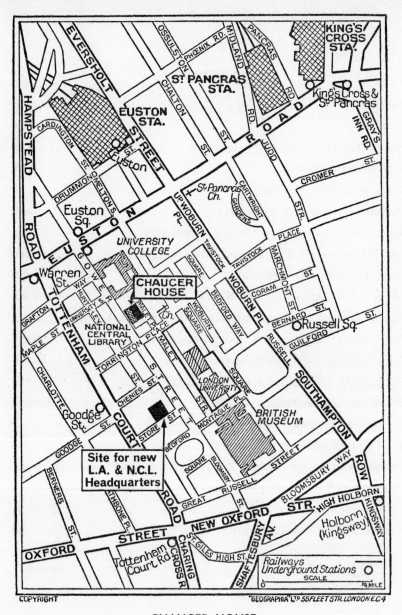

CHAUCER HOUSE

Nearest Tube Station	Goodge Street
Tottenham Court Road Buses	Nos. 1, 14, 24, 29, 39, 73, 134
Woburn Place Buses	Nos. 68, 77, 188, 196

OFFICERS AND COUNCIL

1965

President :

SIR FRANK FRANCIS, K.C.B., Litt.D., M.A., F.S.A., F.L.A.

Immediate Past-President :

F. M. GARDNER, F.L.A.

Past-Presidents :

H. M. CASHMORE, M.B.E., F.L.A.
JAMES WILKIE, M.A., F.R.S.E.
LIONEL R. MCCOLVIN, C.B.E., F.L.A.

Vice-Presidents :

B. S. PAGE, M.A., F.L.A. *(due to retire in 1965).*
E. AUSTIN HINTON, B.A., F.L.A. *(due to retire in 1966).*
MISS F. E. COOK, M.A., F.L.A. *(due to retire in 1967).*

Chairman of Council :

W. S. HAUGH, B.A., D.P.A., F.L.A.

Hon. Treasurer :

W. TYNEMOUTH, F.L.A.

London Councillors :

Due to retire in 1965 :	*Due to retire in 1966 :*
E. V. CORBETT, F.L.A.	R. G. SURRIDGE, F.L.A.
E. P. DUDLEY, F.L.A.	A. J. WELLS, F.L.A.
MISS L. V. PAULIN, M.A., F.L.A.	MISS E. J. WILLSON, F.L.A.

Due to retire in 1967 :

T. E. CALLANDER, F.L.A.
P. W. PLUMB, F.L.A.
W. A. TAYLOR, M.C., F.L.A.

County Councillors :

Due to retire in 1965 :	*Due to retire in* 1966 :
L. L. ARDERN, F.L.A.	G. CHANDLER, M.A., Ph.D.,
E. A. CLOUGH, F.L.A.	F.R.Hist.S., F.R.S.A., F.L.A.
P. HEPWORTH, M.A., F.R.S.A.,	W. S. HAUGH, B.A., D.P.A., F.L.A.
F.L.A.	S. H. HORROCKS, F.L.A.
MISS G. JONES, B.A., F.L.A.	W. HOWARD PHILLIPS, F.L.A.
P. M. WHITEMAN, F.L.A.	M. C. POTTINGER, D.S.C. F.L.A.

Due to retire in 1967 :

J. BEBBINGTON, F.L.A.
F. N. HOGG, D.P.A., F.L.A.
G. E. SMITH, F.L.A.
R. STOKES, F.L.A.
N. TOMLINSON, F.L.A.

Councillors for National, University, College and Medical Libraries :

Due to retire in 1965 :	*Due to retire in* 1966 :
E. H. C. DRIVER, F.L.A.	K. W. HUMPHREYS, B.Litt., M.A.
J. W. SCOTT, B.A., A.L.A.	D. T. RICHNELL, B.A., F.L.A.

Due to retire in 1967 :

A. H. CHAPLIN, B.A., F.L.A.
W. R. LeFANU, M.A., F.S.A.

Councillors for Special Libraries :

Due to retire in 1965 :	*Due to retire in* 1966 :
H. H. GOOM, A.L.A.	K. A. MALLABER, F.L.A.
D. MASON, F.L.A.	J. ROLAND SMITH, F.L.A.

Due to retire in 1967 :

W. ASHWORTH, B.Sc., F.L.A.
T. I. BELL, F.L.A.

Elected by Branches of the Association :
Due to retire in 1965 :

W. CALDWELL, F.L.A. (Northern)

R. F. DREWERY, D.P.A., F.L.A. (Yorkshire)

K. C. HARRISON, M.B.E., F.L.A. (London and Home Counties)

P. HAVARD-WILLIAMS, M.A., A.N.Z.L.A., A.L.A. (Northern Ireland)

R. V. KEYWORTH (Eastern)

A. LONGWORTH, F.L.A. (North Western)

L. M. REES, F.L.A. (Wales and Monmouthshire)

Miss J. M. RHODES, A.L.A. (South Western)

K. A. STOCKHAM, F.L.A. (North Midland)

W. TYLER, F.L.A. (Scottish Library Association)

J. P. WELLS, M.A., F.L.A. (Berkshire, Buckinghamshire and Oxfordshire)

A. WILSON, F.L.A. (West Midland)

Appointed by the Association of Assistant Librarians for 1965 :

J. S. DAVEY, F.L.A.

T. FEATHERSTONE, F.L.A.

J. HOYLE, F.L.A.

MISS J. M. PLAISTER, B.Sc.(Econ.),
F.L.A.

M. J. RAMSDEN, B.A., F.L.A.

The foregoing constitutes the Council.

Secretary :

H. D. BARRY, D.P.A., Barrister at Law

Auditors :

BEEBY, HARMAR & Co., Chartered
Accountants.

Bankers :

BARCLAYS BANK LTD.

Office :

CHAUCER HOUSE, MALET PLACE, W.C.1.

Telephone : Euston 5856 (4 lines). *Telegrams :* "Euston 5856 London ".
Telex : 21897.

Hon. Vice-Presidents :

DR. L. BRUMMEL

H. M. CASHMORE, M.B.E.

DR. LUTHER H. EVANS

R. L. HANSEN

DR. G. HOFMANN

DR. W. MUNTHE

DR. S. R. RANGANATHAN

DR. T. P. SEVENSMA

Honorary Fellows of the Library Association :

E. J. CARTER, B.A.

H. M. CASHMORE, M.B.E.

THE RT. HON. THE EARL OF ELGIN
AND KINCARDINE, K.T.

SIR FRANK FRANCIS, K.C.B., Litt.D.,
M.A., F.S.A.

R. J. GORDON, Hon.M.A.

R. IRWIN, M.A.

L. R. McCOLVIN, C.B.E.

C. B. OLDMAN, C.B., C.V.O.,
Litt.D., M.A., F.S.A.

B. S. PAGE, M.A.

SIR SYDNEY ROBERTS, M.A.

ERNEST A. SAVAGE, LL.D.

J. D. STEWART, M.B.E.

E. SYDNEY, M.C.

WILLIAM BENSON THORNE

P. S. J. WELSFORD, O.B.E.,
F.C.I.S.

COMMITTEES OF THE COUNCIL, 1965

Education :

The President
The Hon. Treasurer
The Chairman of the Council
The Chairman of the Executive
  Committee
D. J. Bryant
W. Caldwell
T. E. Callander (Chairman)
E. V. Corbett
E. A. Clough
E. P. Dudley
E. F. Ferry

H. H. Goom
W. H. Phillips
M. J. Ramsden
Miss J. M. Rhodes
D. T. Richnell
P. H. Sewell
G. E. Smith
R. Staveley
K. A. Stockham
R. G. Surridge
O. S. Tomlinson
P. M. Whiteman

Board of Assessors :

The Chairman of the Education
  Committee
E. A. Clough

K. A. Mallaber
Miss L. V. Paulin
W. Tynemouth (Chairman)

Board of Advanced Studies :

W. Ashworth (Chairman)
S. J. Butcher

D. J. Foskett
R. Irwin

Executive :

The President
The Hon. Treasurer
The Chairman of Council
The Chairman of the Education ;
  Library Research ;
  National, University, College
  and Medical Libraries ;
  Publications ; Public Libraries ;
  and Special Libraries Committees
L. L. Ardern
W. Ashworth

G. Chandler
Miss F. E. Cook
E. V. Corbett
F. M. Gardner
K. C. Harrison
P. Havard-Williams
K. W. Humphreys
Miss L. V. Paulin (Chairman)
M. J. Ramsden
K. A. Stockham

Library Research :

The President
The Hon. Treasurer
The Chairman of Council
The Chairman of the Executive
    Committee
H. M. Cashmore
A. H. Chaplin
E. H. C. Driver
P. Havard-Williams
E. A. Hinton
F. N. Hogg
K. W. Humphreys

Miss G. Jones
R. V. Keyworth
A. Longworth
K. A. Mallaber (Chairman)
Miss J. M. Plaister
P. W. Plumb
M. C. Pottinger
W. A. Taylor
W. Tyler
J. P. Wells
Miss E. J. Willson

National, University, College and Medical Libraries :

The President
The Hon. Treasurer
The Chairman of Council
The Chairman of the Executive
    Committee
L. L. Ardern
A. H. Chaplin
J. S. Davey
R. F. Drewery
E. H. C. Driver

P. Havard-Williams
F. N. Hogg
K. W. Humphreys
W. R. Le Fanu
B. S. Page
D. T. Richnell (Chairman)
J. W. Scott
J. R. Smith
R. G. Surridge

Publications :

The President
The Hon. Treasurer
The Chairman of Council
The Chairman of the Executive
    Committee
The Editor of " The Library
    Association Record "
E. A. Clough
E. V. Corbett
K. C. Harrison
J. Hoyle
R. V. Keyworth

G. Langley
W. R. LeFanu
W. H. Phillips
M. C. Pottinger (Chairman)
Miss J. M. Rhodes
J. W. Scott
J. R. Smith
R. Stokes
N. Tomlinson
A. J. Wells
J. P. Wells

Public Libraries :

The President	E. A. Hinton
The Hon. Treasurer	S. H. Horrocks (Chairman)
The Chairman of Council	J. Hoyle
The Chairman of the Executive	Miss G. Jones
Committee	D. Mason
J. Bebbington	W. H. Milner
G. Chandler	L. M. Rees
Miss B. C. Clark	D. T. Richnell
Miss F. E. Cook	J. C. Sharp
R. F. Drewery	W. A. Taylor
T. Featherstone	C. A. Toase
F. M. Gardner	A. Wilson
P. Hepworth	

Special Libraries :

The President	R. F. Drewery
The Hon. Treasurer	E. H. C. Driver
The Chairman of Council	H. H. Goom
The Chairman of the Executive	K. A. Mallaber
Committee	D. Mason (Chairman)
W. Ashworth	Miss J. M. Plaister
T. I. Bell	P. W. Plumb
H. M. Cashmore	G. E. Smith
G. Crowther	J. R. Smith

JOINT COMMITTEES AND REPRESENTATIVES ON OTHER BODIES

Aberystwyth College of Librarianship Governing Body	B. I. Palmer
British National Bibliography—Council	T. E. Callander
	N. Tomlinson
British National Bibliography—Executive Committee	T. E. Callander
British Records Association Council	H. M. Cashmore
British Standards Institution Committees	
Documentation Standards OC/20	A. J. Walford
Bibliographical References OC/20/1	F. J. Cornell
Indexes and Alphabetical Arrangement OC/20/2	A. J. Walford
Universal Decimal Classification OC/20/4	J. R. Smith
	Vacancy
Abbreviation of Titles OC/20/8	J. L. Thornton

Greek Transliteration OC/20/9/2	Miss B. E. Moon
Arabic Transliteration OC/20/9/3	N. C. Sainsbury
Preparation of Documents for Publication Oc/20/10	J. D. Reynolds
Manufacturers' Trade and Technical Literature S/14	F. J. Cornell
Book Sizes S/21	H. M. Nixon
Proof Corrections S/22	J. D. Reynolds
Terminology (Principles and Co-ordination) USM/4	*Vacancy*
Photographic Aspects of Documentation (International) PHC/12/2	E. F. Patterson
Filing & Storage OEM/2	Miss E. J. Willson
Document Copying Machines OEM/3/7	E. F. Patterson
Council for Educational Advance	D. J. Foskett
Council for Microphotography and Document Reproduction	P. W. Plumb
Ealing Technical College Governing Body	B. I. Palmer
Hospital Libraries Examining Committee, Joint Committee of British Red Cross and St. John	F. M. Gardner
Hospital Libraries Sub-Committee, Joint Committee of British Red Cross and St. John	F. M. Gardner
International Association of Music Libraries	J. H. Davies
International Association of Music Libraries— U.K. Branch	L. W. Duck
International Federation of Library Associations	F. M. Gardner
National Book League Council	F. J. Cornell
	K. C. Harrison
	W. B. Stevenson
National Central Library Board of Trustees	B. S. Page
National Central Library Executive Committee	K. C. Harrison
	J. W. Scott
	K. A. Stockham
National Citizens' Advice Bureaux Committee	C. W. G. Bennett
National Committee on Regional Library Co-operation	J. F. W. Bryon
	W. S. Haugh
National Council of Social Service—Standing Conference on Local History	P. Hepworth
National Council of Social Service—Village Halls Committee	Miss F. R. E. Davies
National Institute of Adult Education—England and Wales	E. Sydney
Polio Research Fund, Committee for Writing and Reading Aids for the Paralysed	P. W. Plumb
Professional Classes Aid Council	D. D. Haslam
Seafarers' Education Service	C. W. Black
Society of Indexers	J. L. Thornton

Unesco National Commission for the U.K.—
  Libraries Advisory Body   S. H. Horrocks
Workers' Educational Association Council   A. Wilson

SENIOR OFFICIALS

Deputy Secretary : D. D. Haslam, F.L.A.

Education Officer : B. I. Palmer, F.L.A.

Publications Officer and Assistant Editor, *L.A. Record* : F. J. Cornell, F.L.A.

Librarian and Information Officer : L. J. Taylor, B.A., A.L.A.

Research Officer: M. Yelland, B.A., A.L.A.

Accountant : C. E. J. Sheppard, A.A.C.C.A.

Assistant Secretary: E. D. Mort, B.Sc.(Econ.).

Editor, *British Humanities Index* : P. Ferriday, B.A.

Editor, *British Technology Index* : E. J. Coates, F.L.A.

Lecturer on loan to the University of Malaya : F. G. B. Hutchings, O.B.E., M.A., F.L.A.

CHAUCER HOUSE

Office Hours : Monday-Friday, 9 a.m.-5 p.m., Saturday, 9 a.m.-12 noon.

Library Hours : Monday, Wednesday and Friday, 9 a.m.-6 p.m., Tuesday and Thursday, 9 a.m.-8 p.m. (no evening opening in August, close at 6 p.m.), Saturday, 9 a.m.-12 noon.

DATES OF COUNCIL MEETINGS, 1965

January 29th   July 9th
April 30th   October 29th

Branches

BERKSHIRE, BUCKINGHAMSHIRE AND OXFORDSHIRE

Officers.

Chairman : H. F. Alexander, M.A. (Bodleian Library).
Vice Chairman : C. Rippon, A.L.A. (Buckinghamshire).
Hon. Secretary : A. E. Day, B.A., F.L.A. (Oxford).
Honorary Treasurer : Miss G. Holroyd, B.A., A.L.A. (Urwick, Orr and Partners).

Committee.

Mrs. P. Heeks, F.L.A. (Berkshire).
S. H. Horrocks, F.L.A. (Reading).
Miss B. P. Hudson, M.A., A.L.A. (Oxfordshire).
Miss C. Kennedy, B.A., A.L.A. (Nuffield College Library, Oxford).
R. J. Key, M.A. (Radcliffe Science Library).
Miss M. Nichols, F.L.A. (Oxford).
D. T. O'Rourke, B.Sc., A.L.A. (Reading University).
C. W. J. Wilson, F.L.A. (A.E.R.E. Harwell).
Branch Councillor: J. P. Wells, M.A., F.L.A. (Oxford).

EASTERN

(The Counties of Norfolk, East Suffolk, West Suffolk, Cambridge, Isle of Ely, and Huntingdon.)

Officers.

Chairman : P. R. Gifford, A.L.A. (Cambridgeshire).
Vice-Chairman : E. F. Ferry, F.L.A. (East Suffolk).
Hon. Secretary : R. V. Keyworth (Huntingdonshire).
Hon. Treasurer : R. H. Fairclough, B.A. (Cambridge University).
Hon. Programme Secretary : F. Fordham, A.L.A. (Bury St. Edmunds).
Hon. Editor : A. A. C. Hedges, F.L.A. (Great Yarmouth).

Committee.

E. Cave, F.L.A. (Cambridge)
D. P. Mortlock, F.L.A. (Norfolk)   } To retire in 1965.
A. V. Steward, F.L.A. (Lowestoft)

P. Hepworth, M.A., F.R.S.A., F.L.A. (Norwich)
Miss M. I. Maynard, A.L.A. (Ipswich)   } To retire in 1966.
J. Thompson, B.A., F.L.A. (University of East Anglia)

W. A. Munford, M.B.E., B.Sc.(Econ.), Ph.D., F.L.A.
Miss J. M. Patterson, A.L.A. (Bury St. Edmonds)   } To retire in 1967.
A. M. Tupling, M.A., F.L.A. (West Suffolk)

LONDON AND HOME COUNTIES

(The Counties of Bedfordshire, Essex, Hertfordshire, Kent, London, Middlesex, Surrey and Sussex.)

Officers.

Chairman : A. C. Jones, F.L.A. (Paddington).
Vice-Chairman : E. P. Dudley, F.L.A. (North Western Polytechnic).
Hon. Secretary : H. Ward, F.L.A. (Stepney).
Hon. Assistant Secretary : D. Jones, F.L.A. (Lewisham).
Hon. Treasurer : E. V. Corbett, F.L.A. (Wandsworth).
Hon. Publications Officer : T. D. F. Barnard, F.L.A. (East Sussex County).
Hon. Publicity Officer : A. W. Ball, F.L.A. (Brighton).

Committee.

General Category :
B. H. Baumfield, F.R.S.A., F.L.A. (Hendon).
H. K. G. Bearman, F.L.A. (West Sussex).
H. G. T. Christopher, A.L.A. (Penge).
A. G. S. Enser, F.R.S.A., F.L.A. (Eastbourne).
G. L. Evans, A.L.A. (Herts. Co.).
Miss S. J. Hardy, F.L.A. (Kent).
J. H. Jones, F.L.A. (Hertfordshire).
A. W. McClellan, A.L.A. (Tottenham).
A. O. Meakin, F.L.A. (Finchley).
K. Newbury, F.L.A. (Coulsdon and Purley).
N. Tomlinson, F.L.A. (Gillingham).
Miss E. J. Willson, F.L.A. (Hammersmith).

Public Libraries Category :
R. D. Rates, F.L.A. (Lewisham).
R. G. Surridge, F.L.A. (Hornsey).

University Library, etc., Category :
Miss J. Bearham, A.L.A. (St. Thomas' Hospital).
I. P. Gibb, B.A., F.L.A. (National Central Library).

NORTHERN

(The Counties of Cumberland, Northumberland, Durham, Westmorland and the North Riding of Yorkshire, excluding Scarborough.)

Officers.

Chairman : K. M. Bramwell, B.A., A.L.A. (I.C.I. Billingham).
Vice-Chairman : Miss A. M. McAulay, B.A., F.L.A. (Durham University).
Hon. Secretary : F. A. Graham, A.L.A. (Vickers-Armstrongs Engineers Ltd.)
Hon. Treasurer : H. H. Douglass, A.L.A. (Durham County).
Immediate Past Chairman : Miss D. Thompson, F.L.A. (Wallsend).
Branch Councillor : W. Caldwell, F.L.A. (Newcastle School of Librarianship).

Committee.

G. R. Fletcher, A.L.A. (Gosforth)
W. Tynemouth, F.L.A. (Newcastle) } To retire in 1966.

Miss M. Wright, F.L.A. (Whitley Bay)
E. W. Kirtley, A.L.A. (Sunderland) } To retire in 1965.

Representing Special Libraries :
Miss M. M. Johnson (C. A. Parsons, Ltd.)   To retire in 1966.
Mrs. J. Robinson (I.C.I. Ltd., HOC. Div.,   To retire in 1965.
    Billingham)

Representing National, University, College and Medical Libraries :
A. T. Hall, A.L.A. (Durham University, Science
    Library)   To retire in 1966.
Dr. W. S. Mitchell, M.A. (University Library,
    Newcastle upon Tyne)   To retire in 1965.

Representing Cumberland and Westmorland Sub-Branch :
D. Bell, A.L.A. (Cumberland).

Representing A.A.L.—N.E. Division :
    P. F. Byrne, A.L.A. (Constantine College of Technology).

As Honorary Vice-President of the Library Association :
    E. Austin Hinton, B.A., F.L.A.

NORTH MIDLAND

(The Counties of Derby (South of a line from Buxton to Dronfield), Nottingham, Lincoln, Rutland, Northampton, Leicester.)

Officers.
President : Dr. R. S. Smith, B.A., F.L.A. (Nottingham University).
Vice-Presidents : J. S. Burden, F.L.A. (Kettering).
                  K. A. Stockham, F.L.A. (Nottinghamshire).
Hon. Secretary : J. N. Taylor, F.L.A. (Nottinghamshire).
Hon. Treasurer : C. G. Browne, A.L.A. (Long Eaton).

Committee.
Miss B. M. Attenborough, F.L.A. (Nottinghamshire).
F. T. Baker, M.A., A.L.A. (Lincoln).
Miss L. I. Edwards, A.L.A. (Nottingham).
D. E. Gerard, B.A., F.L.A. (Nottingham).
P. D. Gratton, F.L.A. (Derbyshire).
C. Hargreaves, A.L.A. (Ilkeston).
E. H. Roberts, F.L.A. (Lindsey & Holland).
G. E. Smith, F.L.A. (Leicestershire).
R. Stokes, F.L.A. (Loughborough School of Librarianship).

NORTH WESTERN

(The Counties of Lancashire and Cheshire, the High Peak District of
Derbyshire and the Isle of Man.)
Officers.
President : D. Mason, F.L.A. (I.C.I. Dyestuffs Division).
Immediate Past President : J. F. W. Bryon, F.L.A. (Eccles).
Vice-President : J. G. McPeake, F.L.A. (Chester).

Hon. Secretary : E. T. Bryant, F.L.A. (Widnes).
Hon. Asst. Secretary : E. H. Mason, F.L.A. (Cheshire).
Hon. Treasurer : G. A. Carter, F.L.A. (Warrington).
Branch Councillor : A. Longworth, F.L.A. (Salford).

Committee.

G. B. Cotton, F.L.A. (Swinton & Pendlebury)
A. R. Hardman, F.L.A. (Bootle)   } To retire in 1966.
J. Hoyle, F.L.A. (Oldham)

R. J. Caul, M.C., F.L.A. (Burnley)
Miss F. E. Cook, M.A., F.L.A. (Lancashire
   County)   } To retire in 1967.
Miss J. A. Downton, M.A., F.L.A. (Preston)

Representing Special Libraries :
D. Kaye, B.A., A.L.A. (I.C.I. Hyde)   To retire in 1966.
B. Howcroft, A.L.A. (C.W.S., Market Research
   Dept.)   To retire in 1967.

Representing National, University, College and Medical Libraries :
A. N. Ricketts, M.A., A.L.A. (Liverpool Univer-
   sity)   To retire in 1966.
C. K. Balmforth, M.A., F.L.A. (Liverpool
   University)   To retire in 1967.

Representing A.A.L. :
Miss S. M. Pinches, A.L.A. (Birkenhead) (Liverpool Division)   To retire in 1966.
D. Harrison, M.A., F.L.A. (Manchester) (Manchester Division)   To retire in 1967.

Hon. Editor, N.W. Newsletter : C. K. Balmforth, M.A., F.L.A.

NORTHERN IRELAND
Officers.

Chairman : L. J. Mitchell, B.A., F.L.A. (Londonderry).
Hon. Secretary : Miss J. B. Webster, M.A., F.S.A., A.L.A. (Queen's Univer-
   sity, Belfast).
Hon. Treasurer : Mrs. I. A. Crawley, F.L.A. (Northern Ireland Command
   Library).
Committee.
Miss A. D. Baillie, B.A., A.L.A. (Co. Down).
I. A. Crawley, F.L.A. (Belfast).
P. Havard-Williams, M.A., A.L.A., A.N.Z.L.A. (Queen's University,
   Belfast).
H. J. Heaney, B.A., A.L.A. (Magee University College, Londonderry).
M. S. Kelly, F.L.A. (Belfast).
Miss M. M. North, B.A., A.T.C.L., A.L.A. (Queen's University, Belfast).
P. J. Quigg, A.L.A. (Belfast).

SOUTH WESTERN
(The Counties of Wiltshire, Somerset, Dorset, Gloucester, Devon, Hampshire, Cornwall and the Isle of Wight.)

Officers.

President : F. S. Green, M.A., F.L.A. (County Seely, Isle of Wight).
Immediate Past President : R. Helliwell, F.L.A. (Winchester).
Chairman : E. A. Clough, F.L.A. (Southampton).
Vice-Chairman : H. Overton, B.Sc. (W. D. & H. O. Wills Ltd., Bristol).
Hon. Secretary : Miss J. M. Rhodes, A.L.A. (Dorset).
Hon. Treasurer : Miss D. Woolley, F.L.A. (Gloucestershire).

Committee.

B. M. Bland, M. Com. (Southampton University)
F. Hallworth, F.L.A., F.R.G.S. (Wiltshire) } To retire in 1965.
G. Scholfield, F.L.A. (Salisbury)

K. Carter, A.L.A. (Dorset)
C. W. Franklin, F.L.A. (Wiltshire) } To retire in 1966.
H. E. Radford, F.L.A. (Bournemouth)

R. E. Grimshaw, F.L.A. (Bristol)
H. Jolliffe, F.L.A. (Swindon) } To retire in 1967.
Miss N. McCririck, B.A., F.L.A. (Somerset)

University and College Representatives : J. Lightbown, M.A., A.L.A. (Bristol University) and I. Rogerson, A.L.A. (North Gloucestershire Technical College).

Special Library Representatives : D. M. Hughes, B.A., F.L.A. (British-American Tobacco Co., Southampton) and H. Overton, B.Sc. (W. D. & H. O. Wills, Ltd., Bristol).

A.A.L. (Bristol & District Division) : G. Langley, B.A., F.L.A. (Bristol).
A.A.L. (Devon and Cornwall Division) : W. A. H. Smith, F.L.A. (Plymouth).
A.A.L. (Wessex Division) : F. W. S. Baguley, A.L.A. (Hampshire).

SCOTTISH LIBRARY ASSOCIATION
(In affiliation with the Library Association.)

Officers.

President : W. R. Aitken, M.A., Ph.D., F.L.A. (Scottish School of Librarianship).
Immediate Past President : W. Scobbie, J.P., A.L.A. (Airdrie).
Vice-Presidents : R. O. MacKenna, M.A., A.L.A. (Glasgow University)—to retire in 1965.
M. K. Milne, A.L.A., F.S.A.(Scot.), (Aberdeen)—to retire in 1966.
J. W. Cockburn, F.L.A. (Edinburgh)—to retire in 1966.
Hon. Secretary : N. R. McCorkindale, D.F.M., A.L.A. (Galashiels).
Hon. Treasurer : W. McK. Murray, A.L.A. (Clackmannan).
Branch Councillor : W. E. Tyler, F.L.A. (Scottish School of Librarianship).

Committee.

Wm. Beattie, C.B.E., LL.D., M.A. (National
  Library of Scotland)
W. H. Brown, F.L.A. (Royal Botanic Garden)
C. S. Minto, F.L.A. (Edinburgh) } To retire in 1965.
Wm. B. Paton, F.L.A. (Lanarkshire)
J. B. Purdie, F.L.A. (Renfrewshire)

R. Hindson, A.L.A. (Colvilles, Ltd.)
H. I. Hunt, F.L.A. (Motherwell and Wishaw)
M. C. Pottinger, D.S.C., F.L.A. (Scottish Central } To retire in 1966.
  Library)

W. A. G. Alison, F.L.A. (Glasgow)
J. W. Forsyth, F.S.A. (Scot.), F.L.A. (Ayr) } To retire in 1967.
R. S. Walker, F.L.A. (Scottish School of Librarian-
  ship)

Representatives of Dundee and Central Scotland Branch : J. R. Barker, M.A.,
  F.L.A. (University Library, Dundee) ; N. Crawford (Arbroath).
Representatives of Edinburgh and East of Scotland Branch : A. Carter, A.L.A.
  (Edinburgh) ; Miss J. P. S. Ferguson, M.A., A.L.A. (Scottish Central
  Library).
Representatives of Glasgow and West of Scotland Branch : Miss A. M. Campbell,
  A.L.A. (Glasgow) ; J. Sharp, F.L.A. (Bute).
Representatives of North of Scotland Branch : S. R. Latham, A.L.A. (Robert
  Gordon's College).

WALES AND MONMOUTHSHIRE

Officers.

President : E. D. Jones, B.A., F.S.A. (National Library of Wales).
Vice-Presidents : Miss K. M. Cooks, F.L.A. (Llandudno).
              Miss E. H. Edwards, F.L.A. (National Museum of Wales).
              Cllr. T. R. Davies (Swansea).
              Thomas Davies, B.Sc., A.I.C. (Haverfordwest).
Chairman : G. Llewellyn, A.L.A. (Breconshire).
Immediate Past Chairman : L. M. Rees, F.L.A. (Swansea).
Vice-Chairman : T. E. Griffiths, B.A., A.L.A. (Caernarvonshire).
Hon. Secretary : D. G. Williams, F.L.A. (Glamorgan).
Hon. Treasurer : J. E. Thomas, F.L.A. (Cardiff).

Committee.

North Wales :	Glyn Davies, F.L.A., F.R.S.A. (Flintshire)	To retire in 1966.
	E. R. Luke, D.P.A., F.L.A., F.R.S.A. (Denbighshire) Miss E. Williams, A.L.A. (Colwyn Bay)	To retire in 1967.
Mid and West Wales :	H. Turner Evans, F.L.A., F.R.S.A. (Carmarthenshire)	To retire in 1965.
	C. W. Newman, B.A., F.L.A. (Radnorshire)	To retire in 1966.
	G. Thomas, B.A., F.L.A. (Cardiganshire)	To retire in 1967.

South Wales : W. J. Collett, F.L.A. (Newport, Mon.)

R. W. Davies, F.L.A. (Pontypridd) } To retire in 1966.

Miss L. E. Gardner, F.L.A. (Rhondda)

D. J. Thomas, A.L.A. (Glamorganshire) } To retire in 1967.

A.A.L. (S. Wales   D. F. Parker, A.L.A. (Monmouthshire).
and Mon. Div.) :   L. Edwards, A.L.A. (Neath).
University and   Miss E. M. Owen, M.A., F.L.A. (Training College,
College Libraries :   Cardiff).

     R. G. Davies, M.A., A.L.A. (University College of Swansea).
Co-opted Members: G. A. Dickman, A.L.A. (Pembrokeshire).

     G. I. John, A.L.A., A.R.P.S. (Aberdare).

     D. O. Jones, F.L.A. (Anglesey).

     H. A. Prestcott, F.L.A. (Llanelly).

WEST MIDLAND

(The Counties of Hereford, Shropshire, Stafford, Warwick and Worcester.)

Officers.

Chairman : H. W. Woodward, A.L.A. (Brierley Hill).
Vice-Chairman : D. Wright, F.L.A. (Birmingham).
Immediate Past Chairman : Mrs. S. M. T. Stone, F.L.A. (The Birmingham Library).
Branch Councillor : A. Wilson, F.L.A. (Dudley).
Honorary Secretary : R. Wright, F.L.A. (Warwickshire).
Honorary Treasurer : A. J. Fox, F.L.A. (Birmingham).
Honorary Editor, Open Access : Miss A. H. Higgs, A.L.A. (Birmingham).
Honorary Membership Secretary : Mrs. M. E. Beaufoy, F.L.A. (Solihull).

Committee.

K. W. Humphreys, B.Litt., M.A. (Birmingham University)

H. D. Budge, F.L.A. (Warwickshire)
E. Hargreaves, F.L.A. (Birmingham) } To retire in 1966.
Miss A. P. Barnes, B.A., F.L.A. (Worcestershire)
A. Shaw Wright, F.L.A. (Herefordshire)

K. J. Rider, F.L.A. (Birmingham)
K. Laugharne, A.L.A. (Redditch College of Further Education)
F. Hughes, F.L.A. (Birmingham School of Librarianship) } To retire in 1965.
R. H. Malbon, F.L.A. (Walsall)
S. Barton, F.L.A. (Staffordshire)

Members nominated for one year :
By the Midland Division of the A.A.L. : D. C. Honour, F.L.A. (Halesowen) and J. R. Dean, F.L.A. (Dudley).

By *the West Midlands Group of the Reference, Special and Information Section:* C. P. Auger, A.L.A. (Lucas Group Research Centre Library) and E. H. C. Driver, F.L.A. (College of Advanced Technology, Birmingham).

By *the University and Research Section, West Midlands:* H. B. Evans, M.A. (Birmingham University) and E. S. Fox, F.L.A. (Birmingham School of Librarianship).

YORKSHIRE

Officers.

Chairman: G. Edmundson, F.L.A. (West Riding).
Vice-Chairman: Dr. D. J. Urquhart, B.Sc. (Nat. Lend. Lib.).
Hon. Secretary: R. G. Benjamin, A.L.A. (Morley).
Hon. Treasurer: C. W. Taylor, F.L.A. (Sheffield).
Hon. Membership Secretary and Hon. Editor, Yorkshire Librarian: K. G. E. Harris, M.A., F.L.A. (Hull).

Committee.

R. B. Bateman, F.L.A. (Leeds Training Coll.)
L. J. Feiweles, B.A., A.L.A. (West Riding) } To retire in 1965.

J. S. Andrews, M.A., A.L.A. (Institute of Education, Leeds University)
R. F. Drewery, D.P.A., F.L.A. (Hull) } To retire in 1966.

C. A. Crossley, F.L.A. (Bradford Institute of Technology)
W. H. Phillips, F.L.A. (Sheffield) } To retire in 1967.

A.A.L.: G. Hare, A.L.A. (Rotherham).
Miss P. Hodgson, A.L.A. (East Riding).
R.S. & I.: Miss J. Spurr, A.L.A. (United Steel).
U. & R.: A. B. Craven, F.L.A. (Leeds).
K. R. Tomlinson, A.L.A. (Halifax College of Further Education).
Youth: Miss E. M. L. Buchanan, A.L.A. (Sheffield).
Mrs. V. Jacques (Bradford).

Groups and Sections
ASSOCIATION OF ASSISTANT LIBRARIANS

Officers.

President : T. M. Featherstone, F.L.A. (Middlesbrough).
Vice-President : Miss J. M. Plaister, B.Sc.(Econ.), F.L.A. (S.E.R.L.S.).
Past President : J. Hoyle, F.L.A. (Oldham).
Hon. Secretary : M. J. Ramsden, B.A., A.L.A. (Nottinghamshire).
Hon. Treasurer : W. S. H. Ashmore, F.L.A. (St. Marylebone).
Hon. Editor : P. D. Gann, F.L.A. (Orpington).
Hon. Education and Sales Officer : J. S. Davey, F.L.A. (N.C.L.).
Hon. Membership Secretary : D. R. Bartlett, B.A., A.L.A. (Nottingham).
Hon. Publications Officer : G. Langley, B.A., F.L.A. (Bristol).
Hon. Conference Secretary : R. Oxley, A.L.A. (Derbyshire).
Hon. Assistant Sales Officer : V. F. Cowmeadow (Edmonton).
Films Officer : W. F. Broome, F.L.A. (Lambeth).

National Councillors.

D. J. Bryant, F.L.A. (Scunthorpe).
A. H. Coles, F.L.A. (Nottinghamshire).
G. Crowther, F.L.A. (Rolls Royce).
F. A. Milligan, M.A., F.L.A. (Herefordshire).
A. P. Shearman, F.L.A. (Sutton & Cheam).
Miss P. A. Trevett, F.L.A. (Hertfordshire).
C. H. Williams, A.L.A. (Liverpool).
T. D. Wilson, F.L.A. (Newcastle Library School).
N. W. Wood, A.L.A. (Cumberland).

Divisional Representatives.

Bristol and District :	P. F. Jackson, A.L.A. (Bristol).
	A. W. Huish, A.L.A. (Swindon).
Devon & Cornwall :	F. Dovey, A.L.A. (Plymouth).
East Midland :	C. C. Williams, A.L.A. (Scunthorpe).
	R. H. Venner, A.L.A. (Nottinghamshire).
Eastern :	F. D. Sayer, A.L.A. (Norwich).
Greater London :	Miss S. M. Bugler, A.L.A. (Middlesex).
	Miss B. Deen (Charing Cross Hospital Medical School).
	Miss J. Nicholson, F.L.A. (Finchley).
	Miss S. A. Wilson, F.L.A. (Finchley).
	P. Davis, A.L.A. (Finchley).
	D. Jones, F.L.A. (Lewisham).
	K. D. Staite, A.L.A. (British Scientific Instrument Research Association).
Kent :	R. H. Searle, A.L.A. (Dartford).
Liverpool :	Miss S. M. Pinches, A.L.A. (Birkenhead).
	Miss M. E. Ehrhardt, B.A., A.L.A. (Birkenhead).
Manchester :	Miss J. M. Ayton, B.A., A.L.A. (Manchester).
	J. D. Lee, F.L.A. (Manchester Library School).
North Eastern :	P. F. Byrne, A.L.A. (Constantine College of Technology, Middlesbrough).
	C. Ferguson, A.L.A. (County Durham).

North Wales :   H. Roberts (Caernarvonshire).
Northern Ireland :   J. P. E. Francis, F.L.A. (Antrim).
Scotland :   Miss A. E. Sutherland, A.L.A. (Edinburgh).
       A. White, A.L.A. (Edinburgh).
South Wales :   G. Thomas, B.A., F.L.A., F.R.S.A. (Cardiganshire Joint Library).
Sussex & Surrey :   Miss P. M. St. J. Brewer (Surrey).
       T. D. F. Barnard, A.L.A. (E. Sussex).
Wessex :   D. G. Dine, A.L.A. (Southampton).
West Midland :   M. F. Messenger, F.L.A. (Shrewsbury).
       J. C. Haywood, F.L.A. (Worcester).
       R. J. Edwards, F.L.A. (Warwickshire).
Yorkshire :   G. Hare, A.L.A. (Rotherham).
       Miss P. Hodgson, A.L.A. (East Riding, Yorks).

CATALOGUING AND INDEXING

Officers.

Chairman : A. H. Chaplin, B.A., F.L.A. (British Museum).
Hon. Secretary : J. C. Downing, F.L.A. (British National Bibliography).

Committee.

C. D. Batty, B.A., F.L.A. (College of Librarianship, Wales).
S. F. Harper, F.L.A. (Willesden).
A. E. Jeffreys, B.A., A.L.A. (University of Keele).
P. R. Lewis, F.L.A. (Board of Trade).
N. F. Sharp, B.A. (British Museum).
C. D. Wort, A.L.A. (Shropshire).

COUNTY LIBRARIES

Officers.

Chairman : E. J. Coombe, F.L.A. (Devon).
Hon. Secretary : K. A. Stockham, F.L.A. (Nottinghamshire).
Hon. Treasurer : Glyn Davies, F.L.A. (Flintshire).

Committee.

England :   Miss F. E. Cook, M.A., F.L.A. (Lancashire)
       Miss L. V. Paulin, M.A., F.L.A. (Hertfordshire)
       D. P. Mortlock, F.L.A. (Norfolk)
Scotland :   W. Mck. Murray, A.L.A. (Clackmannanshire)
Wales :   T. E. Griffiths, B.A., F.L.A. (Caernarvonshire)

       } To retire in 1965.

England :   H. D. Budge, F.L.A. (Warwickshire)
       E. H. Roberts, F.L.A. (Lindsey-in-Holland)
       G. L. Evans, A.L.A. (Hertfordshire)
Scotland :   Miss E. A. Liversidge, F.L.A. (Stirlingshire)
N. Ireland :   L. J. Mitchell, B.A., A.L.A. (Londonderry)

       } To retire in 1966.

England :   E. J. Clark, B.A., B.Com., F.L.A. ⎫
            (Durham)   ⎪
            Miss G. Jones, B.A., F.L.A. (Bucking- ⎪
               hamshire)   ⎬ To retire in 1967.
            P. R. Labdon, F.L.A. (Shropshire)   ⎪
Scotland :   J. Brindle, B.Sc.(Econ.), F.L.A. (Fife)   ⎪
Wales :   D. G. Williams, F.L.A. (Glamorgan) ⎭

The Editor, County Newsletter : E. S. Raven, F.L.A. (Cumberland).

HOSPITAL LIBRARIES AND HANDICAPPED READERS

Officers.

Chairman : R. Sturt, F.L.A. (College of Librarianship, Wales).
Hon. Secretary : Mrs. J. M. Clarke, A.L.A. (St. Thomas' Hospital).
Hon. Treasurer : Miss M. J. Lewis, A.L.A. (School of Librarianship, North-Western Polytechnic).

Committee.

D. Burgess (Lincoln).
Miss M. E. Going, F.L.A. (Kent) *ex-officio.*
G. Thompson, F.L.A. (Leeds).
Miss M. E. Urch, A.L.A. (United Bristol Hospitals).

LIBRARY HISTORY

Officers.

Chairman : Professor R. Irwin, M.A., F.L.A. (University College School of Librarianship and Archives).
Vice-Chairman : Dr. W. A. Munford, M.B.E., B.Sc.(Econ.), F.L.A. (National Library for the Blind).
Hon. Secretary : Miss G. A. Hartnoll, A.L.A. (Commonwealth Relations Office).
Hon. Treasurer : E. P. Dudley, F.L.A. (North-Western Polytechnic School of Librarianship).

Committee.

P. A. Hoare (London Library).
Miss C. R. Lutyens, F.L.A. (Hampstead).
G. K. Scott, F.L.A.

MEDICAL

Officers.

Chairman : W. R. Le Fanu, M.A., F.S.A. (Royal College of Surgeons of England).
Hon. Secretary/Treasurer : E. H. Cornelius, M.A., A.L.A. (Royal College of Surgeons of England).
Hon. Assistant Secretary : Mrs. M. C. Croke, A.L.A. (London School of Hygiene and Tropical Medicine).

Committee.

D. A. Brunning, A.L.A. (Chester Beatty Research Institute).
Miss J. S. Emmerson, M.A. (Newcastle upon Tyne University).

E. Gaskell, B.A., A.L.A. (Wellcome Historical Medical Library).
G. J. Hipkins, B.Sc., F.L.A. (Beecham Research Laboratories, Products Research Division).
Miss E. Lumley Jones, A.L.A. (Welsh National School of Medicine).

REFERENCE, SPECIAL AND INFORMATION
Officers.

Chairman : E. Hargreaves, F.L.A. (Birmingham).
Vice-Chairman : K. A. Mallaber, F.L.A. (Board of Trade).
Hon. Secretary : T. I. Bell, F.L.A. (R.A.E., Farnborough).
Asst. Hon. Secretary : G. E. Hamilton, F.L.A. (Board of Trade).
Hon. Treasurer : J. L. Howgego, B.A., A.L.A. (Guildhall Library).
Hon. Publications and Membership Officer : Miss J. M. Harvey, A.L.A. (Board of Trade).

Committee.

D. W. Bromley, F.L.A. (Sheffield).
H. H. Goom, A.L.A. (G.K.N. Group Research Laboratory).
K. J. Rider, F.L.A. (Birmingham).
F. R. Taylor, F.L.A. (Manchester).
C. A. Toase, A.L.A. (London Borough of Merton).
A. J. Walford, M.A., Ph.D., F.L.A. (Ministry of Defence).
R. C. Wright, A.L.A. (R.A.E., Farnborough).

Group Representatives.

North Midlands : J. G. Ollé, F.L.A. (Loughborough School of Librarianship).
North Western : J. A. Cochrane, F.L.A. (Lancashire).
Northern : D. J. Johnston, B.A., A.L.A. (Sunderland).
South Eastern : F. R. Pryce, A.L.A. (Holborn).
West Midlands : Miss M. W. Chattell, A.L.A. (Walsall).
Western : F. Cochrane, F.L.A. (Royal Military College of Science).
Yorkshire : J. B. Nattriss, B.A., F.L.A. (Leeds).

Honorary Secretaries of R.S.I.S. Standing Sub-Committees

Executive : T. I. Bell, F.L.A. (R.A.E., Farnborough).
Publications : Miss J. M. Harvey, A.L.A. (Board of Trade).
Reference Libraries : Miss C. Williams, A.L.A. (Richmond).
Research : J. B. Cooper, M.A., A.L.A. (Edinburgh University).

Honorary Secretaries of R.S.I.S. Groups.

North Midlands : N. Green, F.L.A. (Nottingham University).
North Western : Miss N. Wright, A.L.A. (U.K.A.E.A.).
Northern : D. J. Johnston, B.A., A.L.A. (Sunderland).
South Eastern : T. M. Rogers, A.L.A. (St. Marylebone).
West Midlands : Miss M. W. Chattell, A.L.A. (Walsall).
Western : J. M. Wood, M.A., F.L.A. (Bristol).
Yorkshire : J. B. Nattriss, B.A., F.L.A. (Leeds).

SOUND RECORDINGS GROUP

Officers.

Chairman : E. Cooper (Enfield).
Vice-Chairman : H. F. J. Currall, F.L.A. (St. Marylebone).
Asst. Hon. Secretary : Miss M. H. Miller, L.R.A.M., A.L.A. (Southwark).
Hon. Secretary : J. W. Howes, F.L.A. (Walthamstow).

Committee.

E. T. Bryant, F.L.A. (Widnes).
F. Jones (Wood Green).
D. G. Williams (Grimsby).

UNIVERSITY AND RESEARCH

Officers.

Chairman : B. S. Page, M.A. (Leeds University).
Deputy Chairman : J. W. Scott, B.A., A.L.A. (University College, London).
Hon. Secretary : D. T. Richnell, B.A., F.L.A. (Reading University).
Hon. Assistant Secretary : P. B. Durey, B.A., F.L.A. (Sussex University).
Hon. Treasurer and Membership Secretary : Miss J. Francis (Richard Thomas and Baldwins Ltd.).

Committee.

A. H. Chaplin, B.A., F.L.A. (British Museum).
E. H. C. Driver, F.L.A. (Birmingham College of Advanced Technology).
S. P. L. Filon, B.Sc., F.L.A. (National Central Library).
R. H. Hill, M.A., F.L.A.
M. B. Line, M.A., F.L.A. (Southampton University).
R. O. MacKenna, M.A., A.L.A. (Glasgow University).
Dr. C. B. Oldman, C.B., M.A., F.S.A., F.L.A.
Dr. R. S. Smith, B.A., F.L.A. (Nottingham University).
S. O. Stewart, M.A., A.L.A. (University of Keele).
Dr. D. J. Urquhart (D.S.I.R., L.L.U.).
K. D. C. Vernon, F.L.A. (Royal Institution).

Scottish Group

Officers.

Chairman : D. W. Doughty, M.A., F.L.A. (St. Andrews University).
Vice-Chairman : D. M. Lloyd, M.A. (National Library of Scotland).
Hon. Secretary : J. V. Howard, M.A., F.L.A. (Dundee University).
Hon. Treasurer : G. R. Pendrill, M.A., F.L.A. (Royal College of Physicians, Edinburgh).

Committee.

J. R. Barker, M.A., F.L.A. (Dundee University).
R. Donaldson, M.A., Ph.D. (National Library of Scotland).
H. J. H. Drummond, M.A. (Aberdeen University).
E. R. S. Fifoot, M.A., A.L.A. (Edinburgh University).
D. MacArthur, M.A., B.Sc., F.L.A. (St. Andrews University).
C. G. Wood, F.L.A. (Andersonian Library).

Colleges of Technology and Further Education Sub-Section

Officers.

Chairman : J. Fry, F.L.A. (Welsh College of Advanced Technology, Cardiff).
Vice-Chairman : E. R. McColvin, A.L.A. (The Polytechnic, Regent Street).
Hon. Treasurer : F. C. Adey, F.L.A. (Colleges of Art and Technology, Leicester).
Hon. Secretary : J. A. Dearden, F.L.A. (Southampton College of Technology).

Committee.

Mrs. J. A. Blackmore, A.L.A. (Hammersmith School of Building and Arts & Crafts).
Miss M. Gwynne-Jones, M.A., A.L.A. (Municipal College of Art, Bournemouth).
R. O. Linden, F.L.A. (South Herts College of Further Education, Barnet).
D. L. Smith, M.A., F.L.A. (College of Technology, Oxford).
E. R. Yescombe, F.L.A. (Northern Polytechnic).

Training Colleges and Institutes of Education Sub-Section

Officers.

Chairman : S. Tillyard, M.A., A.L.A. (Norwich Training College).
Deputy Chairman : C. B. Freeman, M.A., F.L.A. (University of Hull, Institute of Education).
Hon. Secretary : Mrs. O. R. Stokes, F.L.A. (London University Institute of Education).
Hon. Treasurer : Miss V. A. Winn, B.A., A.L.A. (Oxford University Institute of Education).
Hon. Editor : Miss G. G. H. Johnston, M.A., F.L.A. (Kesteven Training College).

Committee.

R. B. Bateman, F.L.A. (City of Leeds College).
E. J. Haywood, A.L.A. (Shoreditch Training College).
W. H. Shercliff, M.A., F.L.A. (Didsbury Training College).
J. D. Dews, M.A., A.L.A. (University of Newcastle upon Tyne).

YOUTH LIBRARIES

Officers.

Chairman : Miss B. C. Clark, F.L.A. (Bristol).
Hon. Secretary : Miss S. G. Bannister, B.A., F.L.A. (Leicestershire).
Hon. Treasurer : D. B. Lomas, A.L.A. (Manchester School of Librarianship).
Hon. Membership Secretary : Miss N. A. Dale, A.L.A. (Lancashire).
Ex-officio member, Retiring Chairman : H. R. Mainwood, A.L.A. (L.C.C.).

Committee.

Miss E. H. Colwell, F.L.A. (Hendon).
Miss L. E. Green, A.L.A. (Nottinghamshire).
Mrs. P. E. Heeks, F.L.A. (Berkshire).
W. H. Milner, M.B.E., F.L.A. (Camberwell).
Miss F. P. Parrott, F.L.A. (Loughborough School of Librarianship).

Past Presidents of The Library Association

Year	President
1877	J. Winter Jones (Director and Principal Librarian of the British Museum).
1878	J. Winter Jones.
1879	H. O. Coxe (Bodley's Librarian).
1880	H. O. Coxe.
1881	His Honour Judge Russell (Master of Gray's Inn).
1882	Henry Bradshaw (Librarian of Cambridge University).
1883	Sir James Picton (Chairman, Liverpool Public Libraries Committee).
1884	J. K. Ingram (Librarian of Trinity College Library, Dublin).
1885	Edward James (Mayor of Plymouth).
1886	E. A. Bond, C.B. (Principal Librarian of the British Museum).
1887	G. J. Johnson (Chairman, Birmingham Public Libraries Committee).
1888	W. P. Dickson (Curator of Glasgow University Library).
1889	Richard Copley Christie (Chancellor of the Diocese of Manchester).
1890	E. Maunde Thompson (Principal Librarian of the British Museum).
1891	Robert Harrison (Librarian of the London Library).
1892	Alexandre Beljame (Professor of English Literature, Sorbonne, Paris).
1893	Richard Garnett (Keeper of the Printed Books, British Museum).
1894	The Most Honourable The Marquess of Dufferin and Ava, K.P., G.C.B.
1895	Lord Windsor.
1896	Alderman H. Rawson (Chairman, Manchester Public Libraries Committee).
1897	Henry R. Tedder (Librarian of the Athenæum).
1898	The Rt. Hon. The Earl of Crawford, K.T.
1899	Alderman James W. Southern, J.P. (Chairman, Manchester Public Libraries Committee).
1900	The Rt. Hon. Sir Edward Fry, P.C.
1901	G. K. Fortescue (Keeper of the Printed Books, British Museum).
1902	W. Macneile Dixon (Birmingham University).
1903	W. Macneile Dixon.
1904	Thomas Hodgkin.
1905	Francis Jenkinson (Librarian, Cambridge University).
1906	Sir William H. Bailey.
1907	Francis T. Barrett (Librarian, Glasgow Public Libraries).
1908	Charles Thomas-Stanford.
1909	Alderman W. H. Brittain, J.P.
1910	Frederic G. Kenyon (Director and Principal Librarian of the British Museum).
1911	Sir John A. Dewar, Bt., M.P.
1912	Frank J. Leslie, C.C.

1913   The Rt. Hon. The Earl of Malmesbury.

1914   Falconer Madan (Bodley's Librarian).

1915   J. Y. W. MacAlister.

1916   J. Y. W. MacAlister.

1917   J. Y. W. MacAlister.

1918   J. Y. W. MacAlister.

1919   G. F. Barwick (Keeper of the Printed Books, British Museum).

1920   The Rt. Hon. J. Herbert Lewis, P.C., M.P. (Parliamentary Secretary, Board of Education).

1921   Alderman T. C. Abbott, J.P. (Chairman, Manchester Public Libraries Committee).

1922   John Ballinger, C.B.E. (Librarian, National Library of Wales).

1923   The Most Honourable The Marquis of Hartington, M.P.

1924   R. S. Rait, C.B.E. (Historiographer Royal of Scotland).

1925   C. Grant Robertson, C.V.O. (Birmingham University).

1926   H. Guppy (Librarian, The John Rylands Library, Manchester).

1927   The Rt. Hon. The Earl of Elgin and Kincardine, C.M.G.

1928   A. D. Lindsay, C.B.E. (Master of Balliol College, Oxford).

1929   Lord Balniel, M.P.

1930   L. Stanley Jast (Chief Librarian, Manchester).

1931   Lt.-Col. J. M. Mitchell, O.B.E., M.C.

1932   Sir Henry A. Miers.

1933   Sir Henry A. Miers.

1934   S. A. Pitt (City Librarian, Glasgow).

1935   E. Salter Davies, C.B.E.

1936   Ernest A. Savage (Chief Librarian, Edinburgh).

1937   William Temple, Archbishop of York.

1938   W. C. Berwick Sayers (Chief Librarian, Croydon).

1939   Arundell Esdaile (Secretary of the British Museum).

1940   Arundell Esdaile.

1941   Arundell Esdaile.

1942   Arundell Esdaile.

1943   Arundell Esdaile.

1944   Arundell Esdaile.

1945   Arundell Esdaile.

1946   H. M. Cashmore (City Librarian, Birmingham).

1947   R. J. Gordon (formerly City Librarian, Leeds).

1948   Charles Nowell (City Librarian, Manchester).

1949   Sir Ronald Forbes Adam, Bt., G.C.B., D.S.O., O.B.E.

1950   His Royal Highness The Duke of Edinburgh.

1951   James Wilkie (Secretary, Carnegie United Kingdom Trust).

1952   Lionel R. McColvin, C.B.E. (City Librarian, Westminster).

1953   S. C. Roberts.

1954   C. B. Oldman, C.B. (Principal Keeper of Printed Books, British Museum).
1955   Sir Philip Morris, C.B.E.
1956   E. Sydney, M.C. (Borough Librarian, Leyton).
1957   Jacob Bronowski.
1958   R. Irwin (Director of School of Librarianship & Archives, University College London).
1959   The Rt. Hon. Earl Attlee, K.G., P.C., O.M., C.H.
1960   B. S. Page (Librarian of the Brotherton Library, Univ. of Leeds).
1961   Sir Charles Snow, C.B.E.
1962   W. B. Paton (County Librarian, Lanarkshire).
1963   J. N. L. Myres (Bodley's Librarian).
1964   F. M. Gardner (Borough Librarian, Luton).

Royal Charter and Bye-laws of
The Library Association

I. (1) VICTORIA, by the Grace of God, of the United Kingdom of Great Britain and Ireland Queen, Defender of the Faith, to all to whom these presents shall come, Greeting :

(2) WHEREAS by a Petition presented unto Us by The Most Honourable Frederick Temple Marquis of Dufferin and Ava, The Right Honourable Robert George Baron Windsor, The Right Honourable Sir John Lubbock, Baronet, Henry Richard Tedder, Esquire, and John Young Walker MacAlister, Esquire ;

(3) It is amongst other things represented :

That in one thousand eight hundred and seventy-seven an Association was established in London called " The Library Association ". That the objects of the Association were, among other things, to promote the establishment of New Libraries ; to endeavour to secure better legislation for Public Libraries ; to unite all persons engaged or interested in library work for the purpose of promoting the best administration of Libraries and to encourage bibliographical research ; and that it would conduce to the welfare of the Association, and to the furtherance of its objects, if the said Association were incorporated by Our Royal Charter.

(4) Now KNOW YE that We have taken into Our Royal consideration the said Petition, and being desirous of promoting the said Association, We have of Our special grace certain knowledge and mere motion given and granted and We do hereby for Us, Our heirs and successors, give and grant that The Most Honourable Frederick Temple Marquis of Dufferin and Ava, Knight of the Most Illustrious Order of St. Patrick, The Right Honourable Robert George Baron Windsor, The Right Honourable Sir John Lubbock, Baronet, Fellow of the Royal Society, Henry Richard Tedder, Esquire, John Young Walker MacAlister, Esquire, and all other persons who, pursuant to this Our Charter, are, or may become Fellows or Members of the Corporation established by this Our Charter in pursuance of the provisions thereof, shall be a body corporate by the name of THE LIBRARY ASSOCIATION, and shall by that name have a perpetual succession and a common seal with a capacity to sue and be sued by their corporate name, and for the purposes of the said Corporation to take, purchase, and hold any personal property, and also notwithstanding the Statutes of Mortmain any real property, provided that the yearly value of such real property shall not at any one time exceed in the whole One thousand pounds, the yearly value of every portion of such real property being for that purpose taken to be the yearly value thereof at the time when it is acquired by the Corporation, with power to sell, grant, demise, mortgage, exchange, and otherwise deal with such real or personal property, or any part thereof, on such terms and in such manner as they may think fit.

And we do hereby declare as follows :—

PRELIMINARY.

II. (1) In the construction of this Our Charter the following words and expressions, unless there is something in the context which is inconsistent with such interpretation, shall have the meanings hereinafter assigned to them, that is to say—

(2) " The Corporation " means the Fellows, Honorary Fellows, and Members of the Library Association, incorporated by this Our Charter.

(3) Words in the masculine gender include the feminine, and words in the singular number include the plural, and in the plural number include the singular.

Purposes and Powers of the Corporation.

III.   The purposes of the Corporation are :—

(1) To unite all persons engaged or interested in library work, by holding conferences and meetings for the discussion of bibliographical questions and matters affecting libraries or their regulation or management or otherwise.

(2) To promote the better administration of Libraries.

(3) To promote whatever may tend to the improvement of the position and the qualifications of Librarians.

(4) To promote the adoption of the Public Libraries Acts in any City, Borough or other district within the United Kingdom of Great Britain and Ireland.

(5) To promote the establishment of reference and lending Libraries for use by the public.

(6) To watch any legislation affecting Public Libraries, and to assist in the promotion of such further legislation as may be considered necessary for the regulation and management or extension of Public Libraries.

(7) To promote and encourage bibliographical study and research.

(8) To collect, collate, and publish (in the form of Transactions, Journals, or otherwise) information of service or interest to the Fellows and Members of the Association, or for the promotion of the objects of the Corporation.

(9) To form, collect, and maintain a Library and Museum.

(10) To hold examinations in Librarianship and to issue Certificates of efficiency.

(11) To do all such lawful things as are incidental or conducive to the attainment of the above objects.

Officers.

IV.   The Officers of the Corporation shall be:—a President, Vice-Presidents, a Treasurer or Treasurers, a Secretary or Secretaries, a Solicitor or Solicitors, an Auditor or Auditors, or such other Officers as may from time to time be prescribed by the Bye-laws of the Corporation for the time being in force.

Membership.

V.   Fellows and Members of the Corporation may be elected in manner provided by any Bye-laws duly made under this Our Charter as hereafter provided.

The Council.

VI.   The Council shall be the governing body of the Corporation, and shall consist of such members as may be from time to time prescribed by the Bye-laws, and subject to such Bye-laws, and in so far as such Bye-laws do not otherwise provide, shall consist of the following persons :—(1) The President, Vice-Presidents, Treasurer, Secretary, Solicitor, and such other Honorary

Officers as may be appointed in accordance with the Bye-laws for the time being in force. (2) Twenty Members or Fellows of the Association at the least, to be annually elected at the Annual General Meeting. The Council shall hold such meetings from time to time as may be prescribed by the Bye-laws for the time being in force, and may hold other meetings as occasion may require, and as the Bye-laws may direct. The first Council of the Corporation shall consist of the persons who, at the date of this Our Charter, are members of the Council of the Library Association. Provided always that any officer who may receive any salary or remuneration for his services from the Corporation, shall not be qualified to be a member of the Council. Subject to the provisions of this Our Charter, or any Bye-law duly made thereunder, the Council shall have the sole management of the income, funds and property of the Corporation and of its affairs, and may do all such things (including the affixing of the common seal of the Corporation to any document) as shall appear to them necessary or expedient in relation thereto.

Executive Committees.

VII.   The Council shall have power to appoint such Executive or other Committees as in their judgment may be necessary, subject to any Bye-law in that behalf which may be made by the Corporation.

The present Officers of the Library Association shall be Officers within the meaning of this Our Charter, and shall be entitled to hold office until the Annual General Meeting of the Corporation held next after the date of this Our Charter.

General and Other Meetings.

VIII.   (1) There shall be a General Meeting of the Corporation within three months after the date of this Our Charter, and such Meeting shall have all the powers of an Annual General Meeting.

(2) An Annual General Meeting of the Corporation shall thereafter be held in every year, at such time and place as the Council shall appoint, but subject to any Bye-law for the time being in force.

(3) Other General Meetings may be held at such times and places as occasion may require, and as the Bye-laws may direct.

(4) The President shall take the chair at any General Meeting at which he is present, and in his absence the Fellows and Members present shall, subject to the Bye-laws, choose one of their number to be Chairman of the Meeting.

(5) The Fellows and Members shall annually elect a President, Vice-Presidents, Treasurer or Treasurers, Secretary or Secretaries, Solicitor or Solicitors, and such other officers as the Bye-laws may direct, and twenty of their number at the least to act as members of the Council.

(6) The Annual or other General Meeting may be adjourned to such time and place as the Meeting may determine, but subject to any Bye-law in that behalf which may be duly made.

Bye-laws.

IX.   Any ten Fellows or Members or Fellows and Members may propose that the Corporation shall make any Bye-law or revoke or alter any existing

Bye-law after giving notice thereof in writing to the Secretary six weeks at least before the Meeting at which such proposal is to be made to the Corporation.

The Council shall have power from time to time to make Bye-laws and from time to time to revoke or alter any Bye-laws theretofore made.

The Bye-laws may provide for all or any of the following matters :—

(a) The carrying out of any of the purposes of the Corporation.

(b) The qualifications, election and classification of the Fellows and Members of the Corporation, and the conditions of Fellowship or Membership, including the contributions to be paid by Fellows and Members to the funds of the Corporation.

(c) The qualifications, election, nomination, appointment, removal, continuance of office, and duties of the Officers or of Members of the Council or of any Executive Committee or Sub-Committee respectively and of all Officers and Servants of the Corporation.

(d) The issuing, renewing and forfeiture of certificates of efficiency and the conditions under which such certificates shall be issued, renewed or forfeited.

(e) Subject to the provisions of this Our Charter, the summoning and holding of and proceedings at General Meetings, including the voting at such Meetings, and the rights and duties of persons present thereat and the quorum necessary to constitute the same.

(f) The summoning and holding of and proceedings at meetings of the Council and of any Executive Committees or Sub-Committees thereof, the quorum at such meetings, and the business, powers and duties of those bodies respectively.

(g) The management of the funds and property of the Corporation.

(h) Any matter connected with, or relating to the affairs or government of the Corporation.

(i) The removal of any Fellow, Member or Associate.

Provided that : (i) The said Bye-laws shall comply with the provisions and directions of this Our Charter ; and (ii) any such Bye-law, and any revocation or alteration thereof shall not take effect unless and until it has been sanctioned by two thirds of the Members present and voting on the question at a duly convened General Meeting, and has been allowed by the Lords of Our Privy Council, of which allowance a Certificate under the hand of the Clerk of Our Privy Council shall be conclusive evidence ; and (iii) The notice convening such General Meeting shall contain a notification that such Bye-law, or such revocation or alteration, will be taken into consideration thereat ; and (iv) The Bye-laws set forth in the Schedule hereto shall, until the same are revoked or altered in manner hereinbefore provided, be deemed to be and shall be the Bye-laws made for the government and regulation of the affairs of the Association.

FUNDS.

X. All property now belonging to or held in trust for, and the benefit of all contracts with the Library Association shall from the date of this Our Charter vest in, and enure for the benefit of, the Corporation, and the Corporation shall pay and discharge all the debts and liabilities of the said Association.

ANNUAL REPORT AND STATEMENT OF ACCOUNTS.

XI. (1) The Council shall once in every year at least prepare a General Report of their proceedings for the year preceding, and attach thereto a duly certified Statement of Accounts and of the Finances of the Corporation, and shall submit the same to the Annual General Meeting of the Corporation.

(2) The accounts of the Corporation shall be audited by an Auditor or Auditors to be appointed each year at the Annual General Meeting. Each Fellow and Member shall be entitled to receive a copy of such Report or Statement.

SUPPLEMENTAL PROVISIONS.

XII. (1) Any act or thing done by the Corporation or by the Council, or by any Committee or Sub-Committee thereof, shall not be invalidated by reason of any vacancy in any office or post in or belonging to the Corporation, or in the Council or in any Committee or Sub-Committee.

(2) A defect in the qualification or election of any person or persons acting as a Member or Members of the Council or of any Committee or Sub-Committee shall not be deemed to vitiate any proceeding of such Council or Committee or Sub-Committee in which he or they has or have taken part, in cases where the majority of Members, parties to such proceedings, are duly entitled to act.

(3) Any document purporting to be certified under the Seal of the Corporation to be a true copy of this Our Charter or of any Bye-laws made thereunder shall, until the contrary is proved, be deemed to be a true copy, and any Bye-laws purporting to be so certified shall, until the contrary is proved, be deemed to have been duly made, sanctioned, and allowed, and to be in force.

(4) Any instrument, which if made by private persons would be required to be under seal, shall be under the seal of the Corporation and signed by the proper Officer of the Corporation. Any notice issued by or on behalf of the Corporation shall be deemed to be duly executed if signed by the proper Officer; but, subject as aforesaid, any appointment made by the Corporation, and any contract, order, or other document made by or proceeding from the Corporation, shall be deemed to be duly executed either if sealed with the seal of the Corporation, and signed by the proper Officer, or if signed by two or more members of an Executive Committee authorized to sign them by a resolution of that Committee, and countersigned by the proper Officer, or if executed in any other manner prescribed by the Bye-laws for the time being in force; but it shall not be necessary in any legal proceeding to prove that the Members signing any such order or other document were authorized to sign them, and such authority shall be presumed until the contrary is proved.

(5) The proper Officer of the Corporation shall be any Officer authorized by the Council to sign such notices and documents as he is required to sign as aforesaid, and it shall not be necessary in any legal proceeding to prove his authority, and such authority shall be presumed until the contrary is proved. The Council may at any time and from time to time, having first obtained the sanction of the majority of the Members and Fellows of the Corporation present, and voting on the question at a General Meeting, of which notice stating the intention to propose the giving of such sanction has

been duly issued, apply for and accept a new and supplemental Charter, or an Act of Parliament, if it appears to the Council that such Charter or Act of Parliament is required for carrying into effect any of the purposes or powers of the Corporation.

In witness whereof We have caused these Our Letters to be made patent.

Witness Ourself at Westminster the Seventeenth day of February in the Sixty-first year of Our reign.

By warrant under the Queen's Sign Manual,

MUIR MACKENZIE.

GREAT
SEAL

BYE-LAWS

(Approved at the Annual General Meeting of the Association on 26th September, 1962, and allowed by Her Majesty's Most Honourable Privy Council on 19th June, 1963.)

INTERPRETATION.

1.—In the interpretation of these Bye-laws the following words and expressions have the following meanings unless inconsistent with the subject or context:

"The Association" means "The Library Association" incorporated by Royal Charter.

"The Charter" means the Royal Charter of incorporation granted to the Association and dated 17th February, 1898.

"Member" means a member of the Association and includes Honorary Fellows, Personal Members, Affiliated Members and Corresponding Personal Members.

"Month" means a calendar month.

Words importing the masculine gender only shall include the feminine, words importing the singular number shall include the plural number and words importing persons shall include corporations.

MEMBERSHIP AND REGISTRATION.

MEMBERS.

2.—The qualifications for election to the respective classes of Members shall be as follows:

(a) *Honorary Fellows.* Persons who in the opinion of the Council have rendered distinguished service in promoting the objects of the Association.

(b) *Personal Members.* Librarians, Bibliographers, Information Officers and other persons connected with the administration of libraries or interested in the objects of the Association.

(c) *Affiliated Members.* Libraries, corporate bodies, societies, and other organizations which maintain or are interested in libraries or information services.

(d) *Corresponding Personal Members.* Persons living outside England, Scotland, Wales, Northern Ireland and the Isle of Man.

METHOD OF ELECTION OF MEMBERS.

3.—The method of election of Members shall be as follows: a proposal giving the candidate's name and qualifications, or the name of the institution, or other organization (as the case may be) signed by two Members, shall be submitted to ballot at the next meeting of the Council, the name of the candidate, institution or other organization (as the case may be) being laid on the table at the meeting. A simple majority of those present shall suffice to elect any candidate. The ballot may be suspended by a majority of those present declaring themselves in favour of such a course. The Council shall have power to reinstate in Membership any Member whose Membership has been cancelled for any reason, and may cause reinstatement to be subject to previous compliance with such conditions as it may determine, including the payment of subscriptions in arrear.

REGISTRATION.

4.—There shall be maintained at the offices of the Association a Register of Librarians who, being Members of the Association, shall be classified as Fellows or Associates of the Association.

5.—(a) The Council shall make regulations for and shall appoint examiners and conduct examinations for the purpose of testing the proficiency of Members desiring to have their names entered on the Register and shall have power to grant exemption from these examinations or parts thereof to Members who have passed such examinations or parts of examinations as may from time to time be considered by the Council to be equivalent to relative parts or the whole of the examinations conducted by the Council.

(b) The Secretary shall cause to be published in the official journal of the Association the names of the successful candidates after each examination.

6.—Any person who is a Member of the Association, and who is engaged in library or bibliographical service, shall be entitled to be entered upon the Register in one or other of the following classes according to his qualifications:

(a) *Associates.* (i) All Members who are Associates of the Association at the date on which these Bye-laws come into operation shall be entered on the Register as Associates.

(ii) A Member who has attained the age of 23 years, has completed three years of library service approved by the Council and has passed the Registration Examination before 1st January, 1964, may be elected as an Associate. Full-time attendance at an approved school of librarianship shall be recognized as equivalent library service for a period not exceeding one year.

(iii) With effect from 1st January, 1964, a Member who has (a) been a Member of the Association for not less than three years (b) completed three years of library service approved by the Council, and (c) passed the Final Examination may be elected as an Associate provided that (unless in the opinion of the Council there are in a particular case exceptional circumstances which would result in hardship) not less than one year of such library service has been served after passing the Final Examination. Full-time attendance at an approved school of librarianship shall be recognized as equivalent library service for a period not exceeding one year.

(b) *Fellows.* (i) All Members who are Fellows of the Association at the date on which these Bye-laws come into operation shall be entered on the Register as Fellows.

(ii) A Member who has attained the age of 25 years, has completed five years of library service approved by the Council and has passed the Final Examination before 1st January, 1964, or (in the case of such persons as the Council may approve) has passed such equivalent examination between 1st January, 1964 and 31st December, 1968, as may be prescribed by the Council may be elected as a Fellow.

(iii) With effect from 1st January, 1964, a Member who has been an Associate for not less than five years and who has completed five years of library service approved by the Council may be elected as a Fellow upon complying with the Regulations with regard to the completion of a thesis.

7.—The Council shall have power to elect as a Fellow of the Association any Member of the Association who although not qualified as an Associate under Bye-law 6 is in the opinion of the Council the author of a published work which represents an outstanding contribution to librarianship or bibliography. Provided that not more than 20 Members shall be included in the Register at any one time as Fellows of the Association elected under this Bye-law.

8.—The Council shall issue to each Fellow and Associate who is entered upon the Register a Certificate of Fellowship or Associateship respectively, but this Certificate shall remain the property of the Association, and shall be returned to the Secretary of the Association, whether demanded or not, if for any reason the holder ceases to be a Member.

9.—Fellows and Associates shall have the right to use the letters F.L.A. and A.L.A. respectively after their names, and may describe themselves as " Chartered Librarians " but only so long as they remain on the Register.

10.—A copy of the Register shall be published in the Year or Hand Book of the Association.

11.—The Council shall have power to reinstate on the Register any Member whose registration has been cancelled, when such Member has been reinstated in Membership under Bye-law 3 and may cause reinstatement to be subject to previous compliance with such conditions as they may determine, including the payment of a further registration fee.

Special Terms of Membership.

12.—The membership of Affiliated Members, and Corresponding Personal Members shall be subject to the following terms and restrictions:

(a) Affiliated Members shall be entitled to appoint one or more representatives being members of their Governing Body or other persons nominated by them and approved by the Council of the Association. Such representatives shall enjoy all the privileges of a Member except that they shall not be entitled to sit for the examinations of the Association, be elected to or remain on the Register of Librarians unless they are themselves Personal Members and that they shall not be entitled as such to vote at General Meetings or at the election of members of the Council.

(b) Corresponding Personal Members shall enjoy all the privileges of a Member except that they shall not be entitled to vote at General Meetings or at the election of Members of the Council or to hold any office in the Association.

13.—All the privileges of membership shall be enjoyed by a Member for his own benefit only and he shall not be entitled to transfer such privileges or any of the benefits derived therefrom to any other person firm company or body.

Reprimand, Suspension and Expulsion of Members.

14.—The Executive Committee shall investigate any complaint made of any action taken by a Member contrary to the aims, objects and interests of of the Association, or of any conduct unbecoming or prejudicial to the profession of librarianship, and if, after such investigation, at which the Member shall be heard, they consider the complaint to be well founded, they shall prefer a formal complaint to the Council and recommend the Council to reprimand or suspend or expel such Member. Notice of such complaint and recommendation, with a copy of this Bye-law, shall be sent to the last registered address of the Member by registered post at least one month before the complaint and recommendation are considered by the Council, and the Member may offer an explanation in writing and shall have the right of being heard before the Council prior to the taking of any decision on the recommendation. The decision of the Council shall be final and binding on the Member. A Member shall be entitled to be represented before the Executive Committee and the Council by Counsel or by a solicitor. The Council may, in its absolute discretion, decide to publish its decision in such newspapers and journals as it shall think desirable.

COUNCIL, COMMITTEES AND OFFICERS.

Constitution of Council.

15.—(a) The affairs of the Association shall, subject to the provisions of the Charter and these Bye-laws, be managed by a Council consisting of the following persons: The President, the Honorary Treasurer, the Immediate Past President, three Vice-Presidents elected in accordance with the provisions of Bye-law 19, nine Councillors whose principal place of business (at the time of election) is within a radius of thirty miles from Charing Cross (hereinafter referred to as "London Councillors"), fifteen Councillors whose principal place of business (at the time of election) is beyond that radius (hereinafter referred to as "Country Councillors"), a Councillor elected by the members of each Branch in accordance with the provisions of Bye-law 19 (hereinafter referred to as "Branch Councillors"), five Councillors to be appointed annually by the Association of Assistant Librarians, six Councillors elected by Members who are employed in National, University, College and Medical Libraries (hereinafter referred to as "University Library Councillors", and six Councillors elected by Members who are employed in special libraries (hereinafter referred to as "Special Library Councillors"). The term "special libraries" means libraries other than Public, National, University, College and Medical Libraries. London Councillors and Country Councillors are hereinafter together referred to as "National Councillors". Only those persons who are eligible to vote at Council elections shall be eligible for election to the Council.

(b) To the Council as constituted in accordance with paragraph (a) of this Bye-law shall be added all Past Presidents serving on the Council on 31st December, 1953, who are willing to serve except that any such Past President who does not attend Council meetings in two consecutive years shall no longer remain a member of the Council.

HONORARY VICE-PRESIDENTS.

16.—The Council shall have power to nominate as Honorary Vice-Presidents twelve persons whose election will in the opinion of the Council be advantageous to the interests and objects of the Association. Honorary Vice-Presidents shall not be members of the Council unless elected under Bye-laws 17-19.

ELECTION OF COUNCIL AND OFFICERS.

17.—On the death or resignation of any elected officer the Council may fill the vacant place for the remainder of the term. On the death or resignation of any Councillor the Council shall fill the vacant place for the remainder of the term by electing the candidate at the preceding Annual Election who received the highest number of votes among the unsuccessful candidates in the division of the Council in which the vacancy occurs. If a Branch Councillor ceases to reside or work within the area of the Branch for which he was elected, he shall cease to be a member of the Council representing that Branch from the end of the current year and his place shall be filled by the appointment of the unsuccessful candidate for that Branch who received the highest number of votes at the preceding election. If there were no contest, the Council may hold an election to fill the vacancy for the remainder of the original term. Any tie between two unsuccessful candidates one of whom would otherwise be appointed under this Bye-law shall be decided by lot by the Chairman of the Council presiding at the first meeting of the Council taking place after the vacancy occurs.

18.—At the annual Election to be held each year for the ensuing year commencing 1st January, the Association shall elect a President, one Vice-President, an Honorary Treasurer, three London Councillors, five Country Councillors, two University Library Councillors, two Special Library Councillors and (every third year) a Branch Councillor in respect of each Branch. The result of the election shall be declared in a list of the candidates in which the names shall be arranged in each division of the Council in order of the number of votes received, the candidates with the highest number of votes to be at the head of the list. The President shall serve for two years, one year as President and one year as Immediate Past President. Vice-Presidents, London Councillors, Country Councillors, University Library Councillors, Special Library Councillors and Branch Councillors shall serve for three years and other members of the Council shall (subject as hereinafter mentioned) serve for one year. Three London Councillors, five Country Councillors, two University Library Councillors and two Special Library Councillors shall retire in every year. All members of the Council qualified to serve on the Council shall be eligible for re-election. In order to start the rotation of Special Library Councillors the two receiving the highest number of votes shall retire in 1964, the two receiving the next highest votes shall retire in 1963 and the two receiving the lowest votes shall retire in 1962 and in the case of University Library Councillors the initial order of retirement shall be determined by lot.

19.—The voting at the election of the Council shall be by postal ballot. The President, Vice-President and Honorary Treasurer shall be nominated by the Council. National Councillors shall be nominated by not less than two qualified voters. Branch Councillors shall be nominated by not less than two qualified voters who are members of the Branch in whose area the candidate resides or works. Only the members of that Branch shall vote for the Branch Councillor. University Library Councillors shall be nominated by not less than two qualified voters who are employed in National, University, College and Medical Libraries, and Special Library Councillors shall be nominated by not less than two qualified voters who are employed in Special Libraries. All nominations by Members must be signed by at least two qualified voters and must be delivered to the Secretary of the Association not later than 15th September in each year and voting papers shall only include valid nominations received by that date. The Secretary shall send by registered post to each candidate notice that he has been nominated, and shall request him to send his written consent to serve upon the Council, if elected. If a nominee declines, or does not reply within 21 days, the Secretary shall inform his nominators of this fact, and the nomination shall not be accepted. If a candidate is nominated for more than one of the following capacities, namely, National Councillor, Branch Councillor, University Library Councillor or Special Library Councillor he shall inform the Secretary of the category for which he wishes to stand but he may not stand for more than one. Voting papers shall be sent not later than 15th November to each voter whose subscription is not in arrear on 1st July in the year of the election, and the Council shall make such regulations as may best enable all qualified voters to record their votes in a secret ballot. The Scrutineers shall declare the result immediately after the counting of the votes and the Secretary shall publish the result immediately by communicating with the candidates by post and by printing the results in the ensuing monthly issue of the official journal. A tie shall be decided by lot by the Chairman of the Council presiding at the first meeting of the new Council.

The Scrutineers at the Annual Election.

20.—The Council shall appoint such number of Members of the Association who are not candidates for election as it may decide to act as Scrutineers at the annual Election and the Council shall determine the procedure to be adopted in the counting of the votes.

Council Vacancies.

21.—The members of the Council may act and exercise all their powers notwithstanding that vacancies for the time being remain unfilled.

22.—A member of the Council may at any time give notice in writing to the Council of his wish to resign and on the acceptance of his resignation by the Council, but not before, his office shall be vacant.

23.—The Association in General Meeting by a resolution requiring a two-thirds majority may remove a member of the Council from his office and thereupon he shall cease to be a member of the Council. A vacancy created by the removal of a member of the Council shall be filled by the Council under Bye-law 17.

24.—Upon the happening of any one or more of the following events as regards a member of the Council his office shall be vacated if the Council so resolve:

(a) If he ceases to be a Member.

(b) If he be expelled or suspended from Membership under the provision of these Bye-laws.

(c) If he be absent from the meetings of the Council for more than four consecutive meetings without the consent of the Council.

(d) If he becomes bankrupt or suspends payment or compounds or makes an assignment of his property for the benefit of his creditors.

(e) If he becomes of unsound mind.

(f) If he be convicted of a felony.

COUNCIL MEETINGS.

25.—Meetings of the Council shall be called by the President, or by the Chairman of the Council, or by the Secretary or on a requisition by any five members of the Council. There shall be not less than four meetings of the Council annually on dates to be fixed by the Council.

26.—The Council may determine the quorum necessary for the transaction of business. Unless otherwise determined twelve members of the Council present in person shall be a quorum.

27.—Except as otherwise provided in these Bye-laws or by the Rules of Procedure as adopted from time to time by the Council every question at meetings of the Council shall be determined by a majority of the votes of the members of the Council personally present and in cases of equality of votes the Chairman shall have a casting vote in addition to his original vote.

28.—All acts done by any meeting of the Council or of any Committee of the Council, or by any persons acting as members of the Council or of such Committee, shall, notwithstanding that it shall be afterwards discovered that there was some defect in the appointment of any member of the Council or Committee or persons acting as aforesaid, or that they or any of them were not qualified, be as valid as if every such person had been duly appointed and was qualified to be a member of the Council or Committee as the case may be.

29.—The Chairman at any meeting of the Council may, with the consent of the meeting, adjourn the meeting from time to time and from place to place but no business shall be transacted at any adjourned meeting other than business left unfinished at the meeting from which the adjournment took place. No notice need be given of an adjourned meeting unless it be so directed in the resolution for adjournment.

STANDING COMMITTEES.

30.—The Council shall appoint Standing Committees, the members of which may be selected from the Council and from the Members to deal with various departments of the Association's work with such powers and under such conditions as from time to time shall be fixed by the Council. Persons who do not belong to the Association may be appointed consultative members of such Committees, but shall not vote upon any question involving expenditure. The Council shall appoint Standing Committees in each year at the first meeting of the new Council.

The Council shall appoint and may from time to time remove the Chairman of the Executive Committee.

31.—The Executive Committee shall report to the Council on matters affecting general policy, legal and parliamentary business, on developments proposed in the work of the Association, and on business not assigned to other Standing Committees; and shall act on behalf of the Council, in an executive capacity, in matters of urgency.

CHAIRMAN OF THE COUNCIL.

32.—At the first meeting of the new Council in each year a Chairman of the Council shall be elected. The Chairman of the Council shall not be eligible for re-election more than twice in successive years. The Chairman of the Council shall take the chair at meetings of the Council and, in the absence of the President, at General Meetings of the Association but in his absence the Meeting shall appoint one of their number being present to take the chair in his place.

THE SECRETARY.

33.—The Secretary shall keep a record of all proceedings, shall draft reports, issue notices, and conduct correspondence and shall have charge of all books, papers and other property belonging to the Association and act generally as the executive officer of the Association.

34.—Proper minutes shall be recorded of all resolutions and proceedings of Meetings of the Council and of the Committees thereof, and every minute signed by the Chairman of the meeting to which it relates or by the chairman of a subsequent meeting shall be sufficient evidence of the facts therein stated.

HONORARY OFFICERS.

35.—The Honorary Officers of the Association shall be the President, the Chairman of the Executive Committee, the Honorary Treasurer and the Chairman of the Council.

FINANCE.

SUBSCRIPTIONS AND FEES.

36.—The Association at its Annual General Meeting shall have power to determine the amounts of all subscriptions, entrance, registration, admission and other fees (except for examination fees) and to increase the same to the following maximum amounts but no higher:

All subscriptions	£15 per annum.
Registration Fee as Associate ..	£10
Transfer Fee to Fellowship ..	£5

The Council, however, shall have power to make regulations admitting persons engaged in library or bibliographical service to Membership or continuing Members in Membership at reduced subscriptions. Such Members shall enjoy all the privileges of Membership, including voting and the receipt of publications usually distributed to Members, except that they may not hold office. The amounts of examination fees shall be determined from time to time by the Council.

37.—Annual subscriptions shall be due and payable in advance on the first day of January in each year. If by 30th June in any year the subscription due by a Member for that year has not been paid, he shall forthwith be suspended from Membership of the Association. If the subscription be paid after 30th June, but before 1st October, the rights and privileges of Membership shall be restored, except that the Member concerned may not vote in the annual election of the Council or of a Branch or Group Committee held during the remainder of that year, and the Member will not be entitled to receive back numbers of THE LIBRARY ASSOCIATION RECORD. If the subscription remains unpaid by 1st October, the defaulter may be removed from Membership of the Association by vote of the Council.

THE HONORARY TREASURER.

38.—The Honorary Treasurer shall receive all moneys due to the Association and shall make such payments as the Council directs and shall supervise the account of all receipts, payments, assets and liabilities of which he shall submit a report to the Annual Meeting and a quarterly statement to the Council. The Council shall make such regulations as it sees fit as regards the payment of accounts and the signature of cheques and other financial documents.

AUDITORS.

39.—At each Annual Meeting an Auditor or Auditors of the Association shall be appointed by the Members present. No person shall be appointed Auditor of the Association who is an Officer of the Association nor unless he is qualified for appointment as Auditor of a Company (other than an exempt private company) under the provisions of Section 161 of the Companies Act, 1948 or any statutory modification or re-enactment thereof.

40.—The Auditor or Auditors of the Association shall have the right of access at all reasonable times to the books and accounts and vouchers of the Association and shall be entitled to require from the Council and Officers of the Association such information and explanation as may be necessary for the performance of the duties of Auditor; and he or they shall sign a certificate at the foot of every Balance Sheet of the Association stating whether or not all his or their requirements have been complied with and shall make a report to the Members on the accounts examined and on every Balance Sheet laid before the Association in General Meeting during his or their tenure of office; and in every such report shall state whether in his or their opinion the balance sheet referred to in the report is properly drawn up so as to exhibit a true and correct view of the state of the Association's affairs as shown by the books of the Association and such report shall be read before the Association in General Meeting.

LOANS.

41.—The Council may borrow money for the purposes of the Association and secure the repayment thereof or the fulfilment of any contract or engagement of the Association in any manner, upon any security, and issue any debentures to secure the same.

RESERVE FUND.

42.—The Council may, out of the moneys of the Association, by way of Reserve Fund, from time to time reserve or set apart such sums as in their judgment are necessary or expedient to be applied at the discretion of the Council to meet claims on or liabilities of the Association, or to be used as a sinking fund to pay off debentures or incumbrances of the Association, or for any other purpose of the Association.

INVESTMENTS.

43.—All funds of the Association not needed immediately for the ordinary purposes of the Association may be invested:

(1) In or upon any of the securities of the government of any country within the Commonwealth, or of the government of any province or state within any such country that has a separate legislature, or of the government of the United States of America; or

(2) In or upon any mortgages or other securities of any municipality, county or district council or local or public authority or board in any country within the Commonwealth, or in any province or state within any such country, or in the United States of America; or

(3) In or upon any mortgages or other securities the capital whereof or a minimum rate of interest or dividend whereon is guaranteed by the government of any country within the Commonwealth, or of any province or state within any such country that has a separate legislature, or by the government of the United States of America; or

(4) In or upon the bonds, debentures, debenture stock or mortgages or the fully paid guaranteed or preference or ordinary stock or shares or ordinary preferred or deferred or other stock or shares of any company incorporated either by Royal Charter or under any general or special Act of the United Kingdom Parliament or any general or special enactment of the legislature of any other country within the Commonwealth or of the United States of America, having an issued and paid up share capital of at least £750,000 or its equivalent at the current rates of exchange, being stocks or shares which are quoted upon a recognized stock exchange in any country within the Commonwealth or the United States of America, and so that in the case of a company having shares of no par value such paid up capital shall be deemed to include the capital sum (other than capital surplus) appearing in the company's accounts in respect of such shares. Provided always that no investment shall be made in any ordinary stocks or shares unless the Company shall have paid dividends thereon at the rate of at least 5 per cent. per annum for at least four years prior to the date of the investment, or, in the case of shares having no par value, the company shall have paid a dividend thereon for at least six years prior to the date of investment, and that the total amount at any time standing invested in investments of the nature described in this sub-paragraph (whether authorized by this sub-paragraph or otherwise) as shown by the books of the Association shall not exceed two-thirds of the total amount at such time standing invested in any of the investments hereby authorized as appearing by such books. Provided always that the Association may accept and (where appropriate) pay for any new shares allotted or offered to the Association in right of shares already held by it or in place thereof whether or not the above limit will thereby be exceeded. For the purpose of valuing the investments authorized by this sub-paragraph and held by the Association the minimum price to be taken for each security shall be the cost price thereof to the Association; or

(5) In the purchase of freehold ground rents or freehold or leasehold land, messuages, tenements and hereditaments within the United Kingdom, provided that as regards leaseholds, the term thereof shall have at least sixty years to run; or

(6) Upon the security of freehold property, freehold ground rents, land charges or rent charges, by way of first mortgage, up to the limit of two-thirds of the value.

44.—The Deeds and Securities of the Association shall be kept in the custody of the Association's Banker on behalf of the Council.

ACCOUNT BOOKS OPEN TO INSPECTION.

45.—The Account Books and Minute Books of the Association shall be open to the inspection of Members of the Council at any reasonable time.

PAID OFFICERS, FEES AND EXPENSES.

46.—The Council shall have power to appoint such paid Officers or Servants as may be necessary for the service of the Association upon such terms as they deem proper. The Council shall also have power to pay the travelling expenses of members of the Council when attending Council and Committee Meetings other than those held at the Annual Meeting, and to pay fees to members of the Council for their services as examiners, or as conductors of correspondence courses. No member of the Council shall be permitted to vote on any matter in which he is financially interested.

INDEMNITY OF COUNCIL AND OFFICERS.

47.—The members of the Council, Secretary and other Officers shall be indemnified by the Association from all losses and expenses incurred by them in or about the discharge of their respective duties, except such as happen from their own respective wilful default.

48.—No member of the Council, Secretary or other Officer shall be liable for any other member of the Council, Secretary or other Officer or for joining in any receipt or document, or for any act of conformity, or for any loss or expense happening to the Association, unless the same happen from his own wilful default.

49.—No portion of the Income or Property of the Association shall be paid or transferred directly or indirectly by way of dividend bonus or otherwise by way of profit to the Members of the Association. Provided always that nothing herein shall prevent the payment in good faith of reasonable and proper remuneration for any services actually rendered to the Association as provided for in Bye-law 46 and elsewhere.

MEETINGS.

CONFERENCES.

50.—The Council shall have power to convene such Conferences as they may see fit of persons interested in the library movement and to approve papers for reading at any such Conference. The Council shall have power to admit persons who are not Members of the Association to any Conference and to fix the fees payable by Members and non-Members for admission to any such Conference provided that the fee payable by Members shall not be more than one-half the fee required from non-Members.

GENERAL MEETINGS.

51.—The Annual General Meeting of Members of the Association shall be held at a time and place to be determined by the Council and this shall be announced not less than three months beforehand. Notices of motion must be sent to the Secretary and delivered not less than two months before the date announced for the Annual Meeting. At least one month's notice of the Annual Meeting shall be sent to each Member entitled to attend and vote at the Meeting. On or before receipt of such notice each Member entitled to attend and vote at the Annual General Meeting shall be sent a copy of the Balance Sheet and Accounts of the Association to be considered at the Meeting and the Auditors' Report thereon.

52.—The Annual General Meeting shall receive and consider the general report of the Council, the Honorary Treasurer's Report and the Balance Sheet and Accounts of the Association with the Auditors' Report thereon and motions of which notice shall have been given in the summons to the meeting. An abstract of the Minutes of the preceding Annual General Meeting containing a transcript of all Resolutions passed shall be read or submitted at the Annual General Meeting.

53.—Upon giving to the Members entitled to attend and vote at General Meetings not less than 21 days written notice the Council may convene an Extraordinary General Meeting whenever they think fit.

54.—On receipt of a requisition from any ten members of the Council or any one hundred Members entitled to vote at General Meetings, the Secretary shall within one calendar month thereafter convene an Extraordinary General Meeting, provided that the purpose for which the Meeting is required be stated in the requisition. No Resolution of an Extraordinary General Meeting convened under this Bye-law shall be deemed carried or shall have effect which has not the support of two-thirds of the Members voting on such Resolution unless at least one-fifth of the Members of the Association entitled to vote at the Meeting have voted thereon.

55.—No business shall be transacted at an Extraordinary General Meeting except such as has been specified in the notice convening it.

56.—Every General Meeting shall be held at such place as the Council shall appoint.

57.—Unless 50 Members be present at the Annual General Meeting within fifteen minutes after the time appointed for the meeting, the meeting shall stand adjourned for a fortnight to be held at the same hour and place or at such other place the Council may determine. On the date to which the meeting was adjourned the meeting shall proceed to business notwithstanding that there may be less than 50 Members present. At an Extraordinary General Meeting unless at least 20 Members are present within fifteen minutes after the time appointed for the meeting, the meeting shall be dissolved.

58.—The Chairman of any meeting may, with the consent of the meeting, adjourn the meeting from time to time, and from place to place as the meeting may determine; but no business shall be transacted at any adjourned meeting other than the business left unfinished at the meeting from which the adjournment took place. No notice need be given of any adjourned meeting unless it is so directed in the resolution for adjournment.

59.—At every General Meeting all questions shall be determined in the first instance by a show of hands.

60.—At any General Meeting, unless a poll on any resolution thereof be demanded by the Chairman or by at least 20 Members present in person and entitled to vote immediately on the declaration by the Chairman of the meeting of the result of the show of hands thereon, a declaration by the Chairman that a resolution is carried or carried by a particular majority, or lost or not carried by a particular majority shall be conclusive, and an entry to that effect in the Minutes of the proceedings of the meeting, shall be sufficient evidence of the fact so declared, without proof of the number or proportion of the votes given for or against such resolution: Provided always that no poll shall be taken as to the election of the Chairman, the appointment of scrutineers, or the adjournment of the meeting, and that notwithstanding a demand for a poll on any resolution the meeting may continue for the transaction of any other business in respect of which a poll has not been demanded. The Members or the Chairman, as the case may be, demanding a poll may nominate not exceeding three Members to act as scrutineers.

61.—If a poll be demanded it shall be taken in such manner as the Chairman of the meeting directs, and the result of the poll shall be deemed the resolution of the General Meeting at which the poll was demanded.

CHAIRMAN'S CASTING VOTE.

62.—In case of equality of votes, either on a show of hands or on a poll, the Chairman shall have a casting vote in addition to his vote as a Member.

VOTING AT GENERAL MEETINGS.

63.—Until 1st January, 1967, only Personal Members of the Association shall be entitled to vote at Meetings of the Association and on the election of Councillors and Officers. As on and from 1st January, 1967, only Fellows and Associates of the Association and those other persons who are Personal Members on 31st December, 1966, and who remain Personal Members shall be entitled to vote at Meetings of the Association and on the election of Councillors and Officers.

64.—On the demand of one-quarter of the Members present, rising in their seats after the Members have voted upon a motion but before the next business has been taken, the Chairman shall rule that the motion be referred to a postal ballot of the Members and that the decision of the postal ballot shall be deemed to be the decision of the meeting. The meeting shall forthwith appoint five of their number as Scrutineers, any three of whom shall be competent to act. The Chairman shall forthwith reduce the resolutions or amendments into the form of alternative propositions so as best to take the sense of the Members on the substantial question or questions at issue. Voting papers setting forth these propositions shall be issued by the Council within fourteen days after the meeting to those Members who were entitled to attend and vote at the meeting and shall be returnable so as to be receivable by the Council within twenty-one days after the meeting. Voting papers shall not be sent to any Member who at the date of the meeting is in arrears of any subscription. The Scrutineers shall meet not less than 21 days nor more than 28 days after the meeting and shall draw up a report of the result of the voting, stating what voting papers have been rejected for non-observance of the notes and directions thereon or disqualified by reason of the voter being in arrear or otherwise ineligible to vote. The report of the Scrutineers shall be conclusive as to the result of the voting and the voting shall take effect from the date of that report. No motion referred to a postal ballot shall be deemed to be carried or have effect unless it has the support of two-thirds of the Members then voting.

65.—No objection shall be made to the validity of any vote at a meeting except at the meeting or poll at which such vote shall be tendered, and every vote not disallowed at such meeting or poll shall be deemed valid. The Chairman of the meeting shall be the sole and absolute judge of the validity of every vote tendered at any meeting or poll.

BRANCHES AND GROUPS.

BRANCHES.

66.—Upon receipt of a request in writing from not fewer than twenty Members of the Association residing in a district the Council may, at their discretion, issue a certificate creating a Branch of the Association. The

Council shall have power to create a Branch notwithstanding that no such request has been received. The certificate shall define the district to be covered by such a Branch, and all Members of the Association residing or working in the district shall be Members of the Branch. No Member shall be a Member of more than one Branch.

67.—No Branch shall levy any charge upon its Members.

68.—A Branch may appoint a Chairman, an Honorary Secretary or Honorary Secretaries, an Honorary Treasurer, and a Committee to manage its affairs, so far as domestic matters are concerned, but shall not take any action, other than by recommendation to the Council, which affects the other Branches, the general conduct of the Association, or the external relations of the Association.

69.—The rules of a Branch, which must not conflict with the Bye-laws of the Association, shall be submitted to the Council for their approval and no amendment or addition shall be valid until approved by the Council.

70.—(a) The Council shall pay to the Branch such proportion of the annual subscriptions received from the Members of that Branch as may from time to time be determined.

(b) Any unexpended balance shall remain at the disposal of the Committee of a Branch unless at any time the accumulated balance shall exceed a sum equal to half the total capitation grant in the previous year, in which case the whole of the unexpended balance shall be refunded to the Council. The Council may, however, authorize the retention of the whole or a part of any such balance if it is needed for some approved purpose.

(c) All money received by the Committee of a Branch shall be expended upon such objects as are provided for in the Charter and Bye-laws and in accordance with the policy of the Council.

(d) The moneys of a Branch shall be kept in a bank nominated by the Committee, in a special account under the name of the Branch.

(e) The Honorary Secretary of a Branch shall forward to the Secretary of the Association, not later than 31st January in each year, an audited statement of accounts together with all books and vouchers for the previous year, and a balance sheet showing the assets and liabilities of the Branch on 31st December.

(f) The Branch Councillor elected in accordance with Bye-law 19 shall be *ex officio* a member of the Branch Committee.

71.—The Honorary Secretary shall also forward a report on the work of the Branch during that year for the information of the Council.

72.—The Council may, at their discretion, revoke a certificate creating a Branch, in which case the certificate shall be forthwith returned to the Secretary of the Association together with all moneys standing to the credit of the Branch after all liabilities have been met. The Council shall, however, give at least twelve months' notice of intention to revoke a certificate creating a Branch. On the dissolution of a Branch, the certificate shall be returned and the balance of moneys paid over as provided above.

Groups.

73.—Upon receipt of a request in writing from not less than fifty Members of the Association for the formation of a Group of the Association, the

Council may at their discretion issue a certificate creating such a Group. The Council shall have power to create a Group notwithstanding that no such request has been received. Any Member may join any two Groups on notifying his desire to the Secretary of the Association. Any Member may join more than two Groups on notifying his desire to the Secretary of the Association and paying, in addition to his normal subscription, an annual subscription equivalent to the amount of the proportion paid by the Council to the additional Group or Groups which he desires to join.

74.—No Group shall levy any charge upon its Members.

75.—A Group may appoint a Chairman, an Honorary Secretary or Honorary Secretaries, an Honorary Treasurer, and a Committee to manage its affairs, so far as domestic matters are concerned, but shall not take any action, other than by recommendation to the Council, which affects the other Groups, the general conduct of the Association, or the external relations of the Association.

76.—The rules of a Group, which must not conflict with the Bye-laws of the Association, shall be submitted to the Council for their approval, and no amendment or addition shall be valid until approved by the Council.

77.—(a) The Council shall pay to the Group such proportion of the annual subscription received from the Members of that Group as may from time to time be determined.

(b) Any unexpended balance shall remain at the disposal of the Committee of a Group unless at any time the accumulated balance shall exceed a sum equal to half the total capitation grant in the previous year, in which case the whole of the unexpended balance shall be refunded to the Council. The Council may, however, authorize the retention of the whole or a part of any such balance if it is needed for some approved purpose.

(c) All money received by the Committee of a Group shall be expended upon such objects as are provided for in the Charter and Bye-laws and in accordance with the policy of the Council.

(d) The moneys of a Group shall be kept in a bank nominated by the Committee, in a special account under the name of the Group.

(e) The Honorary Secretary of a Group shall forward to the Secretary of the Association, not later than 31st January in each year, an audited statement of accounts, together with all books and vouchers for the previous year, and a balance sheet showing the assets and liabilities of the Group on 31st December.

78.—The Honorary Secretary shall also forward a report on the work of the Group during that year for the information of the Council.

79.—The Council may, at their discretion, revoke a certificate creating a Group, in which case the certificate shall be forthwith returned to the Secretary of the Association, together with all moneys standing to the credit of the Group after all liabilities have been met. The Council shall, however, give at least twelve months' notice of intention to revoke a certificate creating a Group. On the dissolution of a Group the certificate shall be returned and the balance of moneys paid over as provided above.

MISCELLANEOUS.

MUSEUM AND LIBRARY.

80.—The Council shall have power to form and maintain a Museum of library appliances and plans, a library, and a bureau of information for Members of the Association and for those interested in library service.

SEAL.

81.—The Council shall provide a Common Seal for the purposes of the Association. The Seal for the time being of the Association shall be kept under such custody and control and used for the purpose of the Association as the Council shall from time to time prescribe.

82.—The Secretary shall affix the Seal with the authority of the Council or of any Committee authorized by the Council to use the Seal and in the presence of two members thereof at least to all instruments requiring to be sealed, and all such instruments shall be signed by such members of the Council and countersigned by the Secretary.

NOTICES, ETC.

83.—All notices, voting papers and circulars required by these Bye-laws to be given or sent to Members shall, unless personally served, be given to the Members having registered addresses in England, Scotland, Wales, Northern Ireland or the Isle of Man, by sending the same to such registered addresses. Provided always that publication of a notice in THE LIBRARY ASSOCIATION RECORD shall constitute good service of such notice upon all Members. Members not having registered addresses in England, Scotland, Wales, Northern Ireland or the Isle of Man shall not be entitled to receive any such documents.

84.—All notices and circulars sent in pursuance of the last preceding Bye-law shall be signed by or have printed at the foot thereof the name of the Secretary or such other person in his place as the Council shall appoint.

85.—Any such notice, voting paper, or circular sent through the post to the registered address of any Member shall be deemed to have been served on him on the day next after that on which it shall have been posted, and in proving such service it shall be sufficient to prove that such notice, voting paper or circular was properly addressed and put into the post office.

86.—Any accidental omission to give notice of any Meetings to or the non-receipt of such notice by any Member or other person entitled to receive the same shall not invalidate the proceedings at any Meeting to be held under the provisions of these Bye-laws.

Annual Election of Officers and Council

REGULATIONS FOR THE CONDUCT OF THE ELECTION ENACTED BY THE COUNCIL UNDER BYE-LAW 19.

In the following regulations the term Members means Members of the Association who are entitled under Bye-law 63 to vote at the Annual Election of Officers and Council

NOTICE OF APPROACHING ELECTION.

1.—Not less than a fortnight before the issue of voting papers a notice shall be sent to all Members, stating :

(1) The date on which voting papers will be issued.

(2) That no voting papers will be sent to Members whose subscriptions have not been paid on or before 30th June.

(3) That if a qualified voter does not receive his voting paper, he must apply for one within a week of the date of issue of the voting papers, after which no voting paper will be issued.

NOMINATIONS.

2.—The Secretary shall send by registered post to each candidate, notice that he has been nominated and shall request him to send his written consent to serve upon the Council, if elected. If a nominee declines, or does not reply within 21 days, the Secretary shall inform his nominators of this fact, and the nomination shall not be accepted. The nominations shall be sent to the Secretary not later than 15th September in each year (Bye-law 19). With this notification that he has been nominated the Secretary shall inform the candidate that he may, if he so wishes, submit, for inclusion in the Nomination Paper, a statement which he must sign and for whose accuracy he will bear full responsibility. This statement, which shall be limited to 50 words, may only contain information limited to the following matters: Present post; previous posts; professional and academic qualifications; summary of activities in connection with the Library Association; summary of other library and bibliographical activities.

QUALIFIED VOTERS.

3.—The Secretary shall on or before 15th November send voting papers to all qualified voters, viz. those whose subscriptions were not in arrear on 1st July.

FORM OF NOMINATION AND VOTING PAPERS.

4.—The Nomination Paper shall be according to Form 5 in the Appendix to these Regulations, and the names of candidates shall be arranged in alphabetical order. The Voting Papers shall be according to Form 6 in the Appendix to these Regulations. The names of all candidates shall be arranged alphabetically on the voting paper under their respective offices. On the Voting Paper candidates shall be described only by their official positions in the libraries in which they hold office or, if retired, last held office, or by their private addresses. On the Nomination Paper retiring councillors who are seeking re-election shall be indicated by an asterisk.

Under each candidate's name shall be printed the statement of information defined above in Paragraph 2.

5.—With each voting paper shall be sent two envelopes (printed as shown in Forms 1 and 2 in the Appendix to these Regulations), together with a circular of instructions which shall be according to Form 4 in the Appendix, and shall specify among other things :

INSTRUCTIONS FOR VOTING.

(1) The latest day upon which voting papers will be received by the Scrutineers.

(2) The place appointed for the counting of the votes.

(3) That the counting will take place at 1 p.m. on the day following the last day for return of papers.

(4) That the proceedings will be open to Members of the Association.

(5) That when the voting paper has been filled up it must be sealed, in the envelope marked " A " (Form 1), and then sealed in the other envelope marked "B " (Form 2), which must bear the signature of the voter. If the voter has voted for a University etc. Libraries Councillor or a Special Libraries Councillor he must also insert the name and description of the library in which the voter is employed.

(6) That, when complete, the paper must be addressed to the Scrutineers and delivered at the office of the Association.

Every third year there will be an election for Branch Councillors. In these years similar nomination and voting papers shall be sent to members and an additional envelope " C " enclosed.

VOTES TO BE COUNTED AT ONE SITTING.

6.—Arrangements shall be made to complete the counting of the votes at a single sitting.

7.—The Scrutineers shall appoint one of their number to preside at the counting of the votes, and his decision on all questions arising in connection with the procedure and the counting shall be final and binding. The Scrutineers, after authority has been obtained from the Hon. Treasurer, shall appoint persons (not being Members), who may be paid for their services, to assist in the counting.

REGISTER OF PERSONS VOTING AND DISQUALIFIED VOTERS.

8.—If any question as to the qualification of any voter be raised it shall be settled by the Scrutineers before the outer (signed) envelopes are opened. If any person who has voted be declared disqualified, the Scrutineers shall mark, on the outer envelope (which must remain unopened) containing his paper, the grounds of disqualification. All such disqualified votes, so marked and with the outer envelopes unopened, shall be submitted to the Executive Committee at their next meeting following the Election, and thereafter shall be preserved by the Secretary for three months from the date of the count ; if by that time a scrutiny has not been demanded, all the papers relating to the Election shall be destroyed by the Secretary. When there is also an election for Branch Councillors the Scrutineers shall satisfy themselves that the voter is a member of the Branch entered upon envelope " C ".

9.—The outer envelopes accepted by the Scrutineers shall be removed from the voting papers under the supervision of the Scrutineers. The inner envelopes shall then be placed in a heap and thoroughly mixed, after which the voting papers shall be taken from the inner envelopes and shall be examined by the Scrutineers, or by Assistants appointed by them. Any voting papers rejected for irregularity shall be placed together in a sealed envelope, and shall be submitted to the Executive Committee at their next meeting following the count, and shall thereafter be retained by the Secretary for a period of three months.

COUNTING.

10.—The voting papers passed as regular shall be counted and numbered consecutively, and the votes therein shall be counted by the Scrutineers or their Assistants by entering the same on prepared lists of the Candidates.

REPORT OF RESULT.

11.—The Scrutineers shall forthwith announce to those present at the counting the total number of votes cast in favour of each candidate, and shall send their certificate of the result (indicating those candidates who are elected and those who are not elected) of the voting to the Secretary, who shall inform the candidates and the members of the Council of the results and shall present the Scrutineers' certificate to the next Meeting of the Association.

SCRUTINY.

12.—A scrutiny shall be held if a requisition to that effect signed by a candidate and his nominators, and supported by five other Members of the Association, be sent to the Scrutineers within four weeks of the count. The requisition must state plainly the grounds on which such scrutiny is demanded.

COUNTING THE VOTES OPEN TO MEMBERS.

13.—Members of the Association shall be entitled to be present at the counting of the votes.

APPENDIX.

FORM 1.

A

THE LIBRARY ASSOCIATION.
ANNUAL ELECTION VOTING PAPER
for Councillors

FORM 2.

B. *The Library Association.*

(*stamp*)

ANNUAL ELECTION.

THE SCRUTINEERS,
The Library Association,
Chaucer House, Malet Place,
London, W.C.1.

....*Signature of Voter*

If the voter has voted for a University etc.
Libraries Councillor or a Special Libraries Councillor he must insert the name of the National,
University, College, Medical or Special library in
which the voter is employed.

....*Library*

which is a National/University/College/Medical/
Special Library
(delete as appropriate)

FORM 3.

C.

The Library Association.

COUNCIL ELECTION
VOTING PAPER
for a Branch Councillor

. . . .
        Branch   *Signature of Voter*

FORM 4.

THE LIBRARY ASSOCIATION,

Chaucer House, Malet Place, London, W.C.1.

19........

DEAR SIR (*or* MADAM),—

Herewith is a Nomination Paper containing the names of those who have been duly nominated for office, or for the seats on the Council, together with a Voting Paper.

If you desire to vote, the voting paper must be marked in accordance with the instructions contained therein, and sealed in the envelope (A) sent herewith. The envelope (A) must then be sealed in the envelope (B).

The outer envelope must be signed at the foot and duly forwarded to the Scrutineers at this address so as to be received by them not later than midday on .... November, 19 .... If you are employed in a National, University, College or Medical Library, or in a Special Library, you are entitled to record additional votes for not more than two councillors for election to represent one or other of these classes of libraries. The term special library means any library which is not a Public, National, University, College or Medical Library. If you do cast these additional votes you must complete the space at the vol. of envelope B giving the name and type of the library in which you are employed.

(*Every third year*.) Your vote for a Branch Councillor can be given on the enclosed form, but only for one of the candidates nominated for the Branch in which you are yourself enrolled as a member. If given elsewhere the vote will be disqualified. This voting paper must be sealed in the envelope (C) which must bear the name of the Branch and be legibly signed by yourself.

The counting will take place *at this address* on the following day, and will begin at one o'clock p.m. Members may be present.

Yours faithfully,

. . . .

Secretary.

Important. Please follow exactly the instructions for completing the Voting Paper and the outer envelope. Any irregularity will mean that your vote is disqualified.

If your signature cannot be identified your vote will be wasted. You are invited to print your name after the signature on the envelope (B)

FORM 5.

THE LIBRARY ASSOCIATION.
ELECTION OF OFFICERS AND COUNCIL

FOR 19. . . .

The following have been Nominated by the Council:
(*Names to be inserted in alphabetical order*.)

AS PRESIDENT.

AS A VICE-PRESIDENT.

AS HONORARY TREASURER.

The following Candidates have been Nominated by Members
(Retiring Members are indicated thus *)

AS LONDON COUNCILLORS.

AS COUNTRY COUNCILLORS.

AS COUNCILLORS FOR NATIONAL, UNIVERSITY, COLLEGE AND MEDICAL
LIBRARIES.

AS COUNCILLORS FOR SPECIAL LIBRARIES.

FORM 6.

THE LIBRARY ASSOCIATION.
ELECTION OF OFFICERS AND COUNCIL FOR 19. . . . .

VOTING PAPER.

In order to vote, a MARK (thus X) must be placed against the names of those Candidates voted for. The whole paper is invalid if more than the required number of names be marked, or if the paper be signed or marked in any way other than as prescribed.

Candidates whose names are printed in *ITALIC CAPITALS* *need not be voted for*, as, there being no competition, they are already *ipso facto* elected.

	Column for vote
AS PRESIDENT.	
AS A VICE-PRESIDENT.	
AS HONORARY TREASURER.	
AS LONDON COUNCILLORS (3 required). DO NOT VOTE FOR MORE THAN THREE. (*Candidates' Names here in alphabetical order.*)	
AS COUNTRY COUNCILLORS (5 required). DO NOT VOTE FOR MORE THAN FIVE. (*Candidates' Names here in alphabetical order.*)	
This section should be used only by members who are employed in National, University, College or Medical Libraries or in Special Libraries.	
AS COUNCILLORS FOR NATIONAL, UNIVERSITY, COLLEGE AND MEDICAL LIBRARIES (2 required). DO NOT VOTE FOR MORE THAN TWO. (*Candidates' Names here in alphabetical order.*)	
AS COUNCILLORS FOR SPECIAL LIBRARIES (2 required). DO NOT VOTE FOR MORE THAN TWO. (*Candidates' Names here in alphabetical order*).	

Index to Royal Charter, Bye-laws and Election Regulations

(Compiled by A. R. HEWITT)

References are to paragraphs and sub-paragraphs—those of the Royal Charter being indicated by roman numerals and those of the Bye-laws by arabic numbers. References to the Election Regulations are preceded by the abbreviation " Reg."

3

Library and Bibliographical Associations of the World

(NOTE.—This list is not complete and includes only those associations who have replied to a questionnaire.)

UNITED KINGDOM

The Library Association, Chaucer House, Malet Place, London, W.C.1.
> *Secretary:* H. D. Barry, D.P.A., Barrister at Law.
> *Official Journal:* Library Association Record (monthly).

Aslib, formerly Association of Special Libraries and Information Bureaux, 3 Belgrave Square, London, S.W.1.
> *Director:* Leslie Wilson, M.A.
> *Official Journals:* Aslib Book List (monthly).
> Journal of Documentation (quarterly).
> Aslib Proceedings (monthly).
> Index to theses accepted for higher degrees in the universities of Great Britain and Ireland (annually).

The Bibliographical Society, Rooms of the British Academy, Burlington Gardens, London, W.1.
> *President:* Sir Frank Francis, K.C.B., M.A., F.S.A., F.L.A.
> *Hon. Secretary:* R. J. Roberts, M.A., A.L.A.
> *Official Journal:* The Library (quarterly).

School Library Association, Premier House, 150, Southampton Row, London, W.C.1.
> *Hon. Secretary:* C. A. Stott, M.B.E., M.A.
> *Official Journal:* The School Librarian and School Library Review.

Circle of State Librarians.
> *Hon. Secretary:* K. J. Spencer, F.L.A., Ministry of Aviation.
> *Asst. Hon. Secretary:* J. R. Brockman, War Office.

Edinburgh Bibliographical Society, c/o National Library of Scotland, George IV Bridge, Edinburgh 1.
> *Secretary:* J. R. Seaton.
> *Treasurer:* J. S. Ritchie.
> *Official Publication:* Transactions.

National Book League, 7 Albemarle Street, London, W.1.
> *General Director:* J. E. Morpurgo, B.A., Litt.D.
> *Secretary and Accountant:* Geoffrey P. Glynn.
> *Official Journal:* Books.

Oxford Bibliographical Society, Bodleian Library, Oxford.
> *Secretary:* Miss M. J. P. Weedon.
> *Official Publication:* Publications of the O.B.S. (formerly Proceedings & Papers) ; Bibliography in Britain (annual).

Cambridge Bibliographical Society, 1 Trinity Street, Cambridge.
> *Hon Secretary:* E. P. Warner.
> *Official Publications:* Transactions (annual) and Monographs (from time to time).

Society for the Bibliography of Natural History, c/o The British Museum (Natural History), London, S.W.7.
Secretary : A. C. Townsend, M.A.
Official Journal : Journal of the Society for the Bibliography of Natural History.

Society of Indexers.
Chairman : G. Norman Knight, M.A., Barrister-at-Law.
Hon. Secretary : E. Alan Baker, F.L.A., 38 Simons Walk, Englefield Green, Egham, Surrey.
Official Journal : The Indexer.

Council for Microphotography and Document Reproduction.
Hon. Director : E. F. Patterson, M.A., A.L.A., c/o Library Association, Chaucer House, Malet Place, London, W.C.1.

Institute of Reprographic Technology, Suite 7, 167 Victoria Street, London, S.W.1.
Secretary : Miss J. I. Bates, A.C.C.S., F.S.C.T.
Publications : Repro (quarterly).

Association of British Theological and Philosophical Libraries.
Hon. Secretary : Miss I. L. Feltwell, A.L.A., National Central Library, Malet Place, London, W.C.1.
Official Publication : Bulletin.

Sconul—Standing Conference of National and University Libraries.
Hon. Secretary : K. W. Humphreys, B.Litt., M.A., Librarian, The University, Edgbaston, Birmingham 15.

Institute of Information Scientists, Ltd.
Hon. Secretary : J. Farradane, " Torran ", Crofton Road, Orpington, Kent.

Classification Research Group.
Hon. Secretary : D. J. Foskett, M.A., F.L.A., Librarian, Institute of Education, University of London, W.C.1.

Association of British Library Schools.
Hon Secretary : Graham Jones, M.A., F.L.A., School of Librarianship, City of Birmingham College of Commerce, Aston Street, Birmingham, 4.

INTERNATIONAL

Asian Federation of Library Associations, c/o Japan Library Association, Ueno Park, Tokyo, Japan.
Secretary-General : Takashi Ariyama.

Fédération Internationale de Documentation (FID), Hofweg, 7, The Hague, Holland.
Acting Secretary-General : W. van der Bruggen.
Official Journal : Revue Internationale de la Documentation (quarterly), FID News Bulletin (monthly).

International Federation of Library Associations, c/o British Museum, London, W.C.1.

President : Sir Frank Francis.

Treasurer : P. Bourgeois, Berne.

Secretary : A. Thompson, 13 Vine Court Road, Sevenoaks.

Official Publications: Actes du Conseil de la FIAB (annual).

IFLA Communications in *Libri* (quarterly) ; Repertoire of the members of the International Federation ; IFLA News/Nouvelles de la FIAB.

United Nations Educational, Scientific and Cultural Organization (Unesco), Place de Fontenoy, Paris 7e, France.

Director-General : René Maheu.

Head, Libraries Division : Carlos Victor Penna.

Official Journals : Unesco Chronicle (monthly) ; Unesco Bulletin for Libraries (bi-monthly) ; Bibliography, documentation, terminology (bi-monthly).

International Association of Music Libraries (I.A.M.L.) (Association Internationale des Bibliothèques Musicales (A.I.B.M.)).

President : Vladimir Fédorov, Paris.

Secretary-General : Dr. Harald Heckmann, Deutsches Musikgeschichtliches Archiv, Ständeplatz, 16, Kassel, Germany.

Official Journal : Fontes artis musicae (three times yearly).

International Association of Agricultural Librarians and Documentalists.

President : F. E. Mohrhardt, Library, U.S. Department of Agriculture, National Agricultural Library, Washington, D.C.

Interim Secretary : Th. P. Loosjes, Library of the State Agricultural University, Wageningen, Holland.

Interim Treasurer : F. C. Hirst, Library, Ministry of Agriculture, Fisheries and Food, London, S.W.1.

International Association of Technical University Libraries (IATUL.)

President : Dr. L. J. van der Wolk, Director, Delft Technical University Library, Delft, The Netherlands.

International Council for Building Research, Studies and Documentation (C.I.B.).

General Secretary : J. de Geus, c/o Bouwcentrum, Weena 700, Rotterdam, P.O. Box 299, The Netherlands.

ARGENTINE

Asociación Latinoamericana de Escuelas y Profesores de Bibliotecología, Corrientes 1723, Buenos Aires.

Secretary : Carlos V. Penna.

Official Publications : Transactions (annual).

Library Schools' Guide in Latin America and Who's Who in the Teaching of Librarianship in Latin America.

Asociacion Argentina de Bibliotecas y Centros de Informacion Cientificos y Tecnicos
Santa Fe 1145, Buenos Aires.
  President : Elisa B. B-Chofen de Mestorino (Mrs.).
  Secretary : Olga E. Veronelli.
Asociación de Bibliotecarios Graduados de la República Argentina, Corrientes 1723 Buenos Aires.
  President : Ricardo J. Lois.
Centro de Estudios Bibliotecologicos, Avenida Corrientes 1723, B.A.
  Secretary : Celina Lecoq.
  Official Publications : Bibliotecología ; Circular Mensual Informativa.
Agrupación de Bibliotecas Populares, calle 46 nro. 483, La Plata, B.A.
  President : Facundo N. Quiroga.

AUSTRALIA

Library Association of Australia, 32 Belvoir St., Surry Hills, N.S.W.
  Hon. General Secretary : R. F. Doust, B.A.
  Official Journal : Australian Library Journal (quarterly).

AUSTRIA

Vereinigung Österreichischer Bibliothekare, Wien I, Josefsplatz 1. (Österreichische National-Bibliothek.).
  Secretary : Dr. Otto Mazal.
  Official Publications : Biblos.
                    Mitteilungen der Vereinigung Österreichischer Bibliothekare.
Verband Österreichischer Volksbüchereien, Wien 8, Schmidgasse 18.
  Presidents : Dr. M. Stickler and Dr. R. Müller.
Wiener Bibliophilengesellschaft, Wien, 5, Kettenbrückengasse 19.
  President : Dr. Walter Sturminger.

BELGIUM

Vlaamse Vereniging van Bibliotheek-, Archief- en Museumpersoneel, Blindestraat 19, Antwerp.
  Secretaries : W. van Cant and J. Martijn.
  Official Journal : Bibliotheekgids (6 nrs.).
Algemeen Sekretariaat voor Katholieke Boekerijen, Cuylitsstraat 27 Antwerp.
  Director : H. Rev. Father Dr. Xaveer De Win.
  Official Publication : Boekengids (monthly).
                    Jeugdboekengids (monthly).
Association des Archivistes et Bibliothécaires de Belgique—Vereniging van Archivarissen en Bibliothecarissen van België, 4, Boulevard de l'Empereur, Bruxelles 1.
  General Secretary : Melle Andreé Scufflaire, conservateur aux Archives générales du Royaume, 78, Galerie Ravenstein, Bruxelles 1.
  Official Journal : Archives et Bibliothèques de Belgique—Archief en Bibliotheekwezen in België.

BRAZIL

Associação Brasileira de Bibliotecarios, Rio de Janeiro.
    President : Lydia de Queiroz Sambaquy.
    1st Secretary : Thaís Caldeira Henriques.
Associação Paulista de Bibliotecários, Caixa Postal 343, Avenida Ipiranga,
    877, 9° andar, s/93-São Paulo.
    President : Alice Camargo Guarnieri.
    1st Secretary : Idelma Freitas Pagliusi.

CANADA

Canadian Library Association (Association Canadienne des Bibliothèques),
    63 Sparks Street, Ottawa.
    Executive Director : Miss Elizabeth H. Morton.
    Official Journal: Canadian Library; the Bulletin of the Canadian
        Library Association; le bulletin de l'Association
        canadienne des Bibliothèques.

CENTRAL AFRICA

Library Association of Central Africa (formerly LA. of Rhodesia & Nyasa-
    land) P.O. Box 1087 Salisbury.
    Hon. Secretary : Mrs. M. Ross-Smith.

CUBA

Asociación Cubana de Bibliotecarios, Carlos III no. 710, Havana.
    Secretary : Olga Céspedes.
    Official Journal : Boletín.

CZECHOSLOVAK SOCIALIST REPUBLIC

Ústřední knihovnická rada ČSSR (Central Library Council of the Czecho-
    slovak Socialist Republic), Prague 1, Klementinum 190.
    Secretary : Jaroslav Lipovský.
    Official Journal : Knihovník (10 issues a year).

DENMARK

Danmarks Biblioteksforening, Mosedalvej 11, Copenhagen, Valby.
    President : R. Lysholt Hansen.
    Secretary : Svend Esbech.
    Official Journal : Bogens Verden.

EGYPT

Egyptian Library Association.
    Secretary : Marcelle Gawly, Librarian, Unesco, Cairo.
    Official Publication : Proceedings (in both English and Arabic).

EIRE

Cumann Leabharlann Na h-Eireann (The Library Association of Ireland),
    46 Grafton Street, Dublin 2.
    Secretary : G. Martin Wheeler, A.C.A., A.C.I.S.
    Official Journal : An Leabharlann : Journal of the Library Association
        of Ireland.

An Leabhar-Cumann (The Book Association of Ireland), 21 Shaw Street, Dublin, 2.

Hon. Secretary : Eoin O'Keeffe, P.C., F.I.I.S.

The Bibliographical Society of Ireland.

Hon. Secretary : Alf MacLochlainn, c/o National Library of Ireland, Dublin.

The Central Catholic Library Association, Inc., 74-75 Merrion Square, Dublin.

Joint Hon. Secretaries : F. F. MacCarthy, M.A., B.E., General P. McMahon.

Hon. Librarian : Reverend R. Burke Savage, S.J.

FINLAND

Suomen Tieteellinen Kirjastoseura—Finlands Vetenskapliga Bibliotekssam-fund (The Association of the Scientific Libraries of Finland), Helsinki, University Library.

President : Prof. Dr. J. Vallinkoski.

Secretary : Miss Rauni Puranen, Phil. Mag., Hallitusk. 1.

Suomen Kirjastoseura (The Library Association of Finland), Helsinki, Museok. 18.

President : Heikki Hosia.

Secretary : Hikka M. Kauppi.

Official Journal : Kirjastolehti (10 issues a year).

Suomen kirjastonhoitajat—Finlands bibliotekarier r.y. (The Librarians of Finland), Helsingin kaupunginkirjasto, Rikhardink 3, Helsinki.

Secretary : Elna Elonheimo.

Official Journal : SK Tiedoittaa (published in Kirjastolehti).

FRANCE

Association des Bibliothécaires français, 65 Rue de Richelieu, Paris IIe.

Secretary : M. J. Lethève.

Official Publications : Bulletin d'Informations (quarterly) ; Listes et fiches critiques (monthly).

GERMANY

Verein Deutscher Bibliothekare e. V., Universitätsbibliothek Munster, 44 Munster/Westf., Postfach 1521.

President : Dr. Gerhard Liebers, Universitätsbibliothek, Munster.

Official Publications : Zeitschrift für Bibliothekswesen und Biblio-graphie ; Jahrbuch der Deutschen Bibliotheken.

Verein der Diplom-Bibliothekare an wissenschaftlichen Bibliotheken e.V., Frankfurt a.M., Zeppelin-Allee 8.

Secretary : Frau Eva Tiedemann.

Verein Deutscher Volksbibliothekare e.V., Bremen-Roonstrasse 57.

President : Bibl. Dir. Dr. Jürgen Eyssen, Hannover.

Official Journal : Bücherei und Bildung.

Verband der Bibliotheken des Landes Nordrhein-Westfalen, Universitäts-
bibliothek, Bochum-Querenburg.
Honorary Secretary : Dr. Horst Röhling.
Official Publication : Mitteilungsblatt.

Deutscher Büchereiverband e.V., Berlin SW 61, Gitschiner Strasse 97-103
Secretary : Klaus-Dietrich Hoffmann.
Communications in : Büchereidienst,
Bücherei und Bildung.

GREECE

Enossis Vivliothikarion tis Hellados (Greek Library Association), Mobil
Library Service, 162 Aristotelousstreet, Athens.
General Secretary : Mrs. Stella Peppa-Xeflouda.

HONG KONG

Hong Kong Library Association.
c/o University Library, University of Hong Kong.

INDIA

Indian Library Association, c/o The Ramakrishna Mission Institute of
Culture, Gol Park, Calcutta 29.
President : Dr. Niharranjan Ray, M.A.(Cal.), D.Lett. and Phil.
(Leiden), F.L.A. (Lond.), M.P.
Secretary : Sri B. Majumdar, M.A., LL.B., Dip.Lib.
Official Journal : The Journal of the Indian Library Association
(Quarterly).

ITALY

Ente Nazionale per le Biblioteche Popolari e Scolastiche, via Michele
Mercati, 4, Roma.
Official Journal : La Parola e il Libro.

Associazione Italiana Biblioteche, Piazza Sonnino, 5, Rome.
President : Dr. Ettore Apollonj.
Secretary : Dr. Maria Valenti.
Official Publication : Bollettino d'informazioni.

JAMAICA

Jamaica Library Association, 2 Tom Redcam Avenue, Kingston 5, Jamaica,
B.W.I.
Hon. Secretary : Miss Sybil M. Jones, A.L.A.
Official Journal : Jamaica Library Association Bulletin.

JAPAN

Japan Library Association, c/o Ueno Library, Ueno Park, Tokyo.
Secretary-General : Takashi Ariyama.
Official Journal : Toshokan Zasshi (Library Journal).

Japan Society of Library Science, Urata Seminar, Faculty of Education,
Tokyo University.
Secretary : Takeo Urata.

LEBANON

The Lebanese Library Association, National Library of Lebanon, Beirut, Lebanon.

President : Me. Ibrahim Maouad.
Secretary : Cheikh Taha El-Waly
Chairman : Ignace A. Khalifé.
Official Publication : Official Journal (annual).

MALAYA

Persatuan Perpustakaan Persekutuan Tanah Melayu.

Acting-President : Mr. C. J. Manuel, University of Malaya, Pantai Valley, Kuala Lumpur, Malaya.

MEXICO

Asociación Mexicana de Bibliotecarios, Apartado Postal No. 13609, Mexico, D.F.

President : Sr. Roberto A. Gordillo.
Vice-President : Sr. Pedro Zamora.
Secretary : Sr. Pablo Velázquez.
Treasurer : Sra. Raisa B. de Datschkovsky.

NETHERLANDS

Nederlandse Vereniging van Bibliothecarissen.

Secretary : Miss V. F. H. E. van Schaick, Frankenstraat 100, Der Haag.
Official Journals : Bibliotheekleven (monthly).
Openbare Bibliotheek (monthly).

Centrale Vereniging voor Openbare Bibliotheken, Centraal Bureau, The Hague, Bezuidenhoutseweg 239.

President : Dr. Anna de Waal, D.Soc.
Secretary-Treasurer : Miss M. Wijnstroom, M.L., F.L.A.
Official Journals : Bibliotheekleven (monthly).
De Openbare Bibliotheek (10 issues a year).

NEW ZEALAND

New Zealand Library Association, 10 Park Street, Wellington, N.1.

Registrar : Doreen G. Bibby.
Official Journal : New Zealand Libraries (monthly).

NIGERIA

Nigerian Library Association, Temporary Secretariat at University of Ibadan, Federal Republic of Nigeria, W.A.

President : Wilfred J. Plumbe, F.L.A.
Secretary : Depo Aramide, F.L.A.
Publications : Nigerian Libraries : Bulletin of the Nigerian L.A.; NILA Newsletter.

NORWAY

Norsk Bibliotekforening, c/o Ringerike Bibliotek, Hönefoss.
> *President* : Helene L. Klemp.
> *Official Journals* : NBF-Nytt and Bok og Bibliotek.

Norsk Bibliotekarlag, Deichmanske bibliotek, H. Ibsensgt. 1, Oslo.
> *President* : Helge Terland.
> *Secretary* : (varies).
> *Official Publications* : Meldinger ; Bibliotek og forskning (Library and Research), ed. by Norsk bibliotekarlag and Norske forskningsbibliotekarers forening.

Norske Forskningsbibliotekarers Forening (Association of Norwegian Research Librarians).
> *Chairman* : Torborg Collin, Ljan (Oslo).
> *Official Publications* : (1) Meldinger (communications appearing irregularly); (2) (in co-operation with Norsk Bibliotekarlag—Norwegian Association of Public Librarians) Bibliotek og Forskning. Årbok. (Libraries and Research Year Book).

PAKISTAN

Pakistan Library Association, Dacca University Library, Dacca-2.
> *Hon. Secretary* : M. S. Khan, M.A., B.L., F.R.Hist.S.
> *Official Journal* : Quarterly Journal of the Pakistan Library Association.

Pakistan Bibliographical Working Group, P.O. Box 534, Karachi-1.
> *President* : Mr. A. R. Ghani.
> *Secretary* : Mr. S. V. Hussain.
> *Treasurer* : Mr. I. H. Kaiser.
> *Official Publications* : Guide to Pakistan libraries, learned and scientific societies and educational institutions; Biographies of Librarians in Pakistan.
> Bibliography of bibliographies.
> Union catalogue of periodicals in Social Sciences held by Libraries in Pakistan.
> Retrospective National Bibliography of Pakistan.

Pakistan Association of Special Libraries, F 35/7 Federal Capital Area, Karachi-19.
> *Hon. Secretary* : S. V. Hussain.

East Pakistan Library Association.
> *President* : Mr. M. S. Khan, M.A., B.L., F.R.Hist.S., c/o Dacca University Library, Dacca.

POLAND

Stowarzyszenie Bibliotekarzy Polskich, ul. Konopczyńskiego 5/7, Warsaw.
Secretary-General : Miss J. Cygańska.
Official Publications :   Przegląd Biblioteczny.
Bibliotekarz.
Poradnik Bibliotekarza.
Informator Bibliotekarza i Ksiegarza.

REPUBLIC OF THE PHILIPPINES

The Bibliographical Society of the Philippines, c/o Unesco National Commission of the Philippines, 1580 Taft Avenue, Manila, Philippines.
Secretary-Treasurer : Filomena C. Mercado.

Philippine Library Association.
President :   Eduardo Malones, cio Manila City Libraries, Philippines.

Association of Special Libraries of the Philippines.
President : Augurio L. Collantes, Joint Legislative-Executive Tax Commission, Manila.

SINGAPORE

Library Association of Singapore, c/o National Library, Stamford Road, Singapore 6.
President : Mrs. Hedwig Anuar.
Vice-President : Mrs. Patricia Lim Pui Huen.
Secretary : Chan Thye Seng.
Treasurer : Miss Kok Poh Yu.
Official Journal : Singapore Library.

SOUTH AFRICA

South African Library Association, c/o Ferdinand Postma Library, Potchefstroom University, Potchefstroom.
President : Prof. H. C. van Rooy.
Hon. Secretary : C. J. H. Lessing.
Official Publications : South African Libraries (quarterly).
S.A.L.A. Newsletter (monthly).

SPAIN

Asociación Nacional de Bibliotecarios, Archiveros y Arqueólogos Delegación de Cataluña y Baleares, Biblioteca Central, Carmen, 47, Apartado 1077, Barcelona.
Secretary : Francisca Solsona Climent, Biblioteca Universitaria, Avda. José Antonio, 585 Barcelona.

Asociación Nacional de Bibliotecarios, Archiveros y Arqueólogos, Biblioteca Nacional, Paseo de Calvo Sotelo 20, Madrid.   Apartado, 14281.
Chairman : Dr. Joaquín Mª de Navascués.
Secretary : Dr. N. Fernández-Victorio.
Official Journal : Boletín.

SWEDEN

Sveriges allmänna biblioteksförening, Nyköping.

   Hon. Secretary : Inga Ström, Stadsbiblioteket, Nyköping.

   Official Journal :   Biblioteksbladet.

Svenska Folkbibliotekarieföreningen.

   Secretary : Erik G. Nyström, Stadsbiblioteket, Vetlanda.

Sveriges vetenskapliga specialbiblioteks förening, Skogsbiblioteket, Stockholm 50.

   Secretary : Ingrid Matérn, Fil. lic.

Tekniska Litteratursällskapet, Ranhammarsvägen 12-14, Bromma 11.

   Secretary : Mrs. Brit Berg.

   Official Publications : Tidskrift för Dokumentation.
   Tekniska Litteratursällskapets bibliografier.
   Tekniska Litteratursällskapets skriftserie.
   Tekniska Litteratursällskapets meddelanden.
   Tekniska Litteratursällskapets handbok.
   Tekniska Litteratursällskapets referenskartotek.

Svenska Bibliotekariesamfundet, Universitetsbiblioteket, Uppsala.

   Secretary : Lennart Grönberg.

SWITZERLAND

Association des bibliothécaires suisses.

   President : Dr. M.-A. Borgeaud, Bibliothèque publique & universitaire, Genève.

   Secretariat : Bibliothèque nationale suisse, Berne.

   Official Journal : Nouvelles de l'Association des bibliothecaires suisses et de l'Association suisse de documentation.

Association Suisse des Bibliothèques d'Hôpitaux. (Veska).

   Secretary : Mme. J. Schmid-Schädelin, Eleonorenstrasse 26, Zürich 32.

TURKEY

Türk Kütüphaneciler Derneği (Turkish Library Association), P.K. 175, Yenişehir-, Ankara.

   Secretary : Özer Soysal.

U.S.A.

American Library Association, 50 East Huron Street, Chicago 11, Ill.

   Executive Director : David H. Clift.

   Official Journal : A.L.A. Bulletin (monthly).

American Merchant Marine Library Association, 45 Broadway, New York, New York 10006.

   Secretary : William P. Bollman, III.

American Theological Library Association.

   Executive-Secretary : Frederick L. Chenery, Episcopal Theological Seminary of the Southwest, 606 Rathervue Place, Austin, Texas, 78705.

American Association of Law Libraries,
Defense Information Office, 120 So. La Salle Street, Chicago, Illinois
60603.
Secretary : Goldie Green Alperin.
Official Journal : Law Library Journal.

Special Libraries Association, 31 East 10th Street, New York 3, New York.
Executive Director : Bill M. Woods.
Official Publications : Special Libraries; Technical Book Review Index ;
Scientific Meetings ; News and Notes.

Medical Library Association, Inc.
Secretary : Miss Betty Withrow, Librarian, Bowman Gray School of
Medicine, Washington-Salem, N.C.
Executive Secretary : Mrs. Helen Brown Schmidt, Medical Library
Association, Inc., 919 North Michigan Avenue,
Chicago 11, Illinois.
Official Journal : Bulletin.

Music Library Association, c/o Music Division, Library of Congress,
Washington 25, D.C.
Executive Secretary : Mr. Ralph Satz, Room 402, 2121 Broadway, New
York 23, N.Y.
Official Publications: Notes and Supplements to Notes.

Association of Research Libraries, 1755 Massachusetts Ave., N.W. Washington D.C., 20036.
Executive Secretary : James E. Skipper.

Bibliographical Society of America, P.O. Box 397, Grand Central Station,
New York 17, New York.
Editor : Robert F. Metzdorf.
Official Publication : Papers.

Catholic Library Association, 461 W. Lancaster Avenue, Haverford,
Pennsylvania.
Executive Director : M. Richard Wilt.
Official Publication : Catholic Library World.

URUGUAY
Asociación de Bibliotecarios del Uruguay.
Secretary : Ema S. de Mateos, Ateneo de Montevideo, Plaza Libertad,
Casilla de Correo 1415, Montevideo.

VENEZUELA
Colegio de Biblioteconomos y Archivistas de Venezuela, Apartado 6283,
Caracas.
President : Guillermo Luna.
Vice-President : Carmen Montes.
Secretary : Mary Herrera.
Treasurer : María de Lourdes García.

YUGOSLAVIA

Savez društava bibliotekara F.N.R. Jugoslavije (Union des Associations des Bibliothécaires de la R.F.P. de Yougoslavie), Beograd, Terazije 26.

Secretary : Emil Popović.

Official Publications : Bibliotekar (Beograd).
Vjesnik bibliotekara Hrvatske (Zagreb).
Bilten Društva bibliotekara Bosne i Hercegovine i Narodne biblioteke (Sarajevo).
Knjižnica (Ljubljana).

GHANA

Ghana Library Association, P.O. Box 4105, Accra, Ghana.

President: G. M. Pitcher, F.L.A.

Secretary: S. A. Afre, A.L.A.

Library Co-operation and the National Central Library

The National Central Library (Librarian and Secretary to the Trustees, S. P. L. Filon, T.D., B.Sc., F.L.A.), Malet Place, London, W.C.1.

The Library was founded by the late Dr. Albert Mansbridge in 1916 as the Central Library for Students and reconstituted as the National Central Library in 1930. Its original purpose, was to provide books for organized classes for adult education, but it is now not only a great lending library itself but also the recognized centre for the loan, between libraries of all kinds both within Great Britain and abroad, of books for study which cannot be obtained in any other way. It has also become the main centre for the supply of information about books both for national and for international purposes, and for the recording and allocation of duplicate books to suitable libraries at home and abroad, and for dealing with reciprocal offers of exchange material from libraries abroad.

The Library is the centre of the national system of library co-operation which now covers the whole of the country, and acts as a clearing house between the Regional Library Bureaux (see below). It is also the centre for co-operation and the inter-lending of books between university and specialized libraries and those of Government departments and research and industrial organizations.

Applications are accepted for all types of books and periodicals with the following exceptions : those in print at 25s. or less ; books which are available at the applicant's own library ; works of fiction (unless required for research purposes) ; and books required continuously for examination purposes (i.e. text-books). In addition applications are not accepted from the Regional systems for British books listed in *B.N.B.* from January, 1959 ; this restriction does not apply to libraries having direct relations with the N.C.L. The Library lends books from its own stock, and in addition is in a position to obtain from other libraries a very large percentage of those books which it is unable to supply itself. It has, in this way, access to many volumes as well as many thousand sets of periodicals. Among the books supplied are highly specialized or expensive books and periodicals which the borrowing library would not be justified in buying, even if it could afford to do so ; scarce and out-of-print books ; foreign books of which no copies are available in this country ; back volumes of periodicals ; and photographic copies of manuscripts and rare printed books which cannot be lent.

In order to fulfil its functions, the Library has made itself responsible for the gradual building up of a great national union catalogue of the non-fiction books in all the important lending libraries in the British Isles including the many specialized libraries (known as " Outlier Libraries ") from which it is able to borrow books. This catalogue, in all its sections, already contains about two million entries.

Scotland : The Scottish Central Library (Librarian, M. C. Pottinger, D.S.C., F.L.A.), Lawnmarket, Edinburgh, 1.

Ireland : The Irish Central Library for Students, 53 Upper Mount Street, Dublin.

London Union Catalogue Management Committee (Hon. Secretary, L. F. Hasker, F.L.A.), National Central Library, Malet Place, London, W.C.1.

Northern Regional Library Bureau, Central Library, New Bridge St., Newcastle-upon-Tyne, 1 (Hon. Secretary, E. Austin Hinton, B.A., F.L.A.), covering the counties of Cumberland, Durham, Northumberland, Westmorland and the Cleveland District of Yorkshire.

Regional Library Bureau (West Midlands), Reference Library, Birmingham, 1, covering the counties of Herefordshire, Shropshire, Staffordshire, Warwickshire, and Worcestershire.

Welsh Regional Library Bureaux. Aberystwyth Bureau, National Library of Wales (Hon. Secretary, E. D. Jones, B.A.) : Cardiff Bureau, Central Library, Cardiff (Hon. Secretary, J. E. Thomas, F.L.A.). These Bureaux cover the whole of Wales and Monmouthshire.

South-Eastern Regional Library Bureau (Hon. Secretary, W. J. Hill, F.L.A.), National Central Library, Malet Place, London, W.C.1, covering the counties of Bedfordshire, Berkshire, Buckinghamshire, Essex, Hertfordshire, Kent, Middlesex, Surrey and Sussex.

East Midlands Regional Library Bureau, Central Library, Bishop Street, Leicester (Hon. Secretary, W. R. M. McClelland, F.L.A.), covering the counties of Cambridge, Derby, Huntingdon, Leicester, Lincoln, Norfolk, Northampton, Nottingham, Rutland and Suffolk.

North-Western Regional Library Bureau, Central Library, St. Peter's Square, Manchester, 2 (Hon. Secretary, D. I. Colley, F.L.A.), covering the counties of Cheshire, Lancashire and the Isle of Man.

Yorkshire Regional Library System (Hon. Secretary, C. W. Taylor, F.L.A., Central Library, Sheffield).

South-Western Regional Library Bureau (Hon. Secretary, A. J. I. Parrott, F.L.A.), Central Public Library, Bristol, covering the counties of Cornwall, Devon, Dorset, Gloucester, Hampshire (including the Isle of Wight), Oxford, Somerset and Wiltshire.

The object of the regional systems is to meet demands for books locally, as far as possible, and so minimize the calls upon the National Central Library and lessen the time required to supply a book. Libraries participating in regional systems apply for books to their local Regional Bureaux, which forward to the National Central Library those applications with which they are unable to deal. Libraries in Scotland and Ireland send applications through the Scottish and Irish Central Libraries respectively. No applications should be sent direct by members of the public to any of the Central Libraries or Regional Bureaux, but only through their own librarians. There is no charge for borrowing books through the National Central Library or a Regional Bureau beyond, in some cases, the cost of postage both ways.

Statistical and other information about the Regional Systems, the " Outlier ", University and other libraries in co-operation with the National Central Library, and other co-operative projects, will be found in the Annual Reports of the National Central Library and of the Regional Library Systems.

The Library Association Carnegie Medal

The Library Association Carnegie Medal is awarded annually for an outstanding book for children by a British subject published in the United Kingdom during the preceding year.

At the end of each year recommendations for the award are invited from members of the Library Association, who are asked to submit a preliminary list of not more than three titles from which the Committee makes a final selection.

The award is open to works of non-fiction as well as fiction and the choice is based upon consideration of all the following points :

FICTION. (i) Plot; (ii) Style; (iii) Characterization; (iv) Format (including production and illustrations, if any).

NON-FICTION. (i) Accuracy; (ii) Method of presentation; (iii) Style; (iv) Format, etc.

The following is a list of L.A. Carnegie Medal winners since the institution of the award.

LIST OF LIBRARY ASSOCIATION CARNEGIE MEDAL WINNERS

1936 RANSOME, Arthur. *Pigeon post* (Cape).

1937 GARNETT, Eve. *The family from One End Street* (Muller).

1938 STREATFEILD, Noel. *The circus is coming* (Dent).

1939 DOORLY, Eleanor. *Radium woman* (Heinemann).

1940 BARNE, Kitty. *Visitors from London* (Dent).

1941 TREADGOLD, M. *We couldn't leave Dinah* (Cape).

1942 " B.B. " (D. J. WATKINS-PITCHFORD). *The little grey men* (Eyre & Spottiswoode).

1943 Prize withheld as no book considered suitable.

1944 LINKLATER, Eric. *The wind on the moon* (Macmillan).

1945 Prize withheld as no book considered suitable.

1946 GOUDGE, Elizabeth. *The little white horse* (Univ. London Press).

1947 DE LA MARE, Walter. *Collected stories for children* (Faber).

1948 ARMSTRONG, R. *Sea change* (Dent).

1949 ALLEN, Agnes. *The story of your home* (Faber).

1950 FOULDS, Elfrida Vipont. *The lark on the wing* (O.U.P.).

1951 HARNETT, Cynthia. *The wool-pack* (Methuen).

1952 NORTON, Mary. *The borrowers* (Dent).

1953 OSMOND, Edward. *A valley grows up* (O.U.P.).

1954 FELTON, Ronald Oliver ("Ronald Welch"). *Knight Crusader* (O.U.P.).

1955 FARJEON, Eleanor. *The little bookroom* (O.U.P.).

1956 LEWIS, C. S. *The last battle* (Bodley Head).

1957   MAYNE, W.   *A grass rope* (O.U.P.).
1958   PEARCE, Ann Philippa.   *Tom's midnight garden* (O.U.P.).
1959   SUTCLIFF, Rosemary. *The lantern bearers* (O.U.P.).
1960   CORNWALL, Dr. I. W.   *The making of man* (Phoenix House).
1961   BOSTON, Lucy M.   *A stranger at Green Knowe* (Faber).
1962   CLARKE, Pauline.   *The twelve and the genii* (Faber).
1963   BURTON, Hester.   *Time of trial* (O.U.P.).

The Library Association Kate Greenaway Medal

The Library Association Kate Greenaway Medal is intended to recognize the importance of illustrations in children's books. (An article on the award appeared in the RECORD for December, 1955.) It is awarded to the artist who, in the opinion of the Library Association, has produced the most distinguished work in the illustration of children's books during the preceding year.

The artist must be a British subject, and the work published in the United Kingdom.

Books intended for older as well as younger children are included, and reproduction will be taken into account.

Recommendations for the award are invited from members of the L.A., who are asked to submit a preliminary list of not more than three titles.

1955　Prize withheld as no book considered suitable.
1956　ARDIZZONE, Edward. *Tim all alone* (O.U.P.).
1957　DRUMMOND, V. H. *Mrs. Easter and the storks* (Faber).
1958　Prize withheld as no book considered suitable.
1959　STOBBS, W. *Kashtanka* and *A bundle of ballads* (O.U.P.).
1960　ROSE, Gerald. *Old Winkle and the seagulls* (Faber).
1961　MAITLAND, Antony. *Mrs Cockle's cat* (Constable).
1962　WILDSMITH, Brian. *A.B.C.* (O.U.P.).
1963　BURNINGHAM, John. *Borka: the adventures of a goose with no feathers* (Cape).

The Library Association Wheatley Medal

The Library Association Wheatley Medal is awarded annually for an outstanding index published during the preceding year.

Printed indexes to any type of publication may be submitted for consideration but the award is limited to indexes compiled by individuals and not by corporate bodies.

Recommendations for the award are invited from members of the L.A. and the Society of Indexers.

The final selection is made by a committee consisting of representatives of the L.A. and the Society of Indexers.

The award is made to the compiler of the winning index who must be British and the book must have been published in the United Kingdom.

1962　MACLAGAN, Michael. *Clemency Canning* (Macmillan).
1963　DICKIE, J. M. *How to catch trout*. Third ed. (W. & R. Chambers).

Other Awards and Prizes

L.A. Prize Essay

£25 offered annually for an essay. Closing date for entries : 1st *April,* 1965. (Full details will be found in the November, 1964 Record, page 479.)

Francis J. Thacker Scholarship

£40 offered for a thesis on a subject of the candidate's choice within the fields of Bibliography or Library Administration, Method, Policy or History. (Full details from the Hon. Secretary, West Midland Branch.)

J. D. Stewart Travelling Bursary

£50 to be made available annually for the purpose of helping a student-librarian to visit an overseas country to study librarianship. Applications not later than 1st January for year in question. (Full details from the Hon. Secretary, London and Home Counties Branch.)

Cyril Barnard Memorial Prize

Awarded triennially for an outstanding contribution to medical librarianship. (Further details from Hon. Secretary, Medical Section.)

Charles Nowell Memorial Prize

Awarded annually by the North Western Branch.

Scottish Library Association Prizes

(i) Two annual prizes for merit to Registration Course student at the Scottish School of Librarianship.
(ii) The Ewart Prize.

Northern Branch Essay Competition

Annual competition for a prize of £10.

Albert Cawthorne Prize

Awarded annually to the student who obtains the highest marks in the Part I Examination. (Further details from the Secretary of the L.A.)

F. Robinson Bequest

A bequest " for the purpose of periodically rewarding the originality and inventive ability of librarians and others, interested persons or firms in connection with devising new and improved methods in library technology and any aspect of library administration ". (Conditions of the award will be found in the October 1964 Record, page 450.)

SYLLABUS

OF THE

PROFESSIONAL EXAMINATIONS

CONDUCTED BY

THE LIBRARY ASSOCIATION

(TOGETHER WITH INFORMATION

ON FACILITIES FOR STUDY

AND TRAINING)

INTRODUCTION

The Library Association was incorporated by Royal Charter, and amongst the purposes of the Association, as set out in the Charter are the following :

"To promote whatever may tend to the improvement of the position and qualifications of Librarians."

"To hold examinations in Librarianship and to issue Certificates of efficiency."

Accordingly, the Association maintains a Register of Chartered Librarians and admits its members thereto when they furnish proof of their suitability.

The proof is furnished by passing the Part II Examination of the Library Association and by producing evidence of the completion of three years' approved library service. A Member who meets these conditions may apply to be elected to the Register as an Associate of the Library Association.

The Syllabus is related to full-time tuition at Schools of Librarianship and although the Library Association does not *require* candidates to undergo a course of study in preparation for the examinations, Members wishing to qualify are strongly advised to do so as the standard required of candidates is a high one. There are no age limits for sitting the examinations. Information on study facilities is given on pages 55-75.

An announcement is published in the *Library Association Record* for February and August giving all the information required by prospective candidates for the examinations. The results are published in the September and March *Library Association Record* for the Summer and Winter Examinations respectively.

Sets of the examination papers are available for purchase as separate publications, price 3s. a set for each session of examinations.

POST-GRADUATE SYLLABUS: A special note

At the meeting of the Council held on October 30th, 1964, it was decided to introduce a post-graduate syllabus to operate from 1966 onwards. Details of this syllabus appeared in the *L.A. Record* for January 1965 : but at the time of going to press the regulations and other administrative details were not available. They will be published in the *L.A. Record* from time to time, and incorporated in the *Students' handbook* for 1966-67.

Graduates will no longer be granted exemption from the Part I examination but will be expected to qualify by means of the Post-graduate syllabus.

REGULATIONS AND SYLLABUS OF PROFESSIONAL EXAMINATIONS

Regulations governing the Professional Examinations and admission to the Register of Chartered Librarians

1. Admission to the Register of Chartered Librarians maintained by the Library Association is obtainable by members of three years' standing on passing the Association's Examinations and producing evidence of having completed at least three years' approved full-time library service,[1] and of having reached an appropriate minimum standard[2] in a language other than English, or in science.[3]

2. The professional examinations consist of:

   (*a*) The Part I Examination
   (*b*) The Part II Examination.

3. The examinations are open only to members of the Library Association.

4. A candidate for the Part I Examination must produce evidence that he has (*a*) passed the General Certificate of Education in five subjects, of which one must be in English Language and two must be at Advanced level ; *or* (*b*) obtained a Scottish Certificate of Education in five subjects, of which one must be English and three at Higher grade ; *or* (*c*) obtained the Northern Ireland Senior Grammar School Certificate with five passes, of which one must be English and two at Advanced level ; *or* (*d*) as a temporary measure, passed the Entrance Examination of the Library Association ; *or* (*e*) passed

---

[1] At least one year of such service must come after completing the Part II Examination. For conditions of approval of library service, see p. 54. Whole-time paid service normally consists of 35 hours per week, but in the case of libraries where normal hours of work are less than this, consideration will be given to each case. The salary received must be appropriate, in the opinion of the Council, to the work. Whole-time attendance at an approved school of librarianship will be recognized as equivalent library service for a period not exceeding one year.

[2] The minimum acceptable standard shall be the General Certificate of Education at "O" level, *or* a First Class Certificate in the Intermediate Stage of the Royal Society of Arts, *or* the Student Stage II Certificate of the Institute of Linguists.

[3] The list of sciences recognized by the Council is as follows :

Mathematics	Biology
Pure mathematics	Botany
Additional mathematics	Zoology
Applied mathematics	Human anatomy, physiology and
Pure and applied mathematics	hygiene
Mathematics and theoretical mechanics	Human biology and hygiene
General science	Elementary physiology
Additional general science	Physics with electronics
Physics	Elementary aeronautics
Chemistry	Agricultural science
Physics with chemistry	Horticultural science
Mechanics	Rural biology
Geology	Physiology and hygiene

the First Professional Examination of the Library Association ; *or* (*f*) obtained such other general educational certificate as the Council shall from time to time accept as being of equivalent standard.[1] [2]

5. No candidate will be admitted to the Part II Examination until he has passed the Part I Examination or has obtained exemption therefrom.

6. Exemption from the Part I Examination may be granted to Members who hold a degree of a university in the United Kingdom, or, at the discretion of the Board of Assessors, to Members who hold (*a*) professional qualifications by examination of an overseas library association ; or (*b*) a diploma in librarianship or a degree from an overseas university. Documentary evidence of degree or professional qualification is required, and an exemption fee of £2 10s. is payable.

7. Exemption from the Part I and Part II Examinations will be granted upon the submission of documentary evidence and payment of the exemption fee to members who have passed the main Diploma Examination (i.e. Part I of the Post-Graduate Diploma Course) of the London University School of Librarianship and Archives or the equivalent examination of Sheffield University, or of Queen's University, Belfast.

8. The examinations are held in the Summer and Winter of each year. The dates of the examinations will be published in the February and August issues of the *Library Association Record*.

9. Candidates for examinations must apply to the Secretary on the appropriate form on or before March 31st for entrance to the Summer Examinations, and on or before September 30th for the Winter examinations. A form of entry will be provided upon application, which must be returned, together with the fee, any necessary documents and two stamped self-addressed envelopes. Applications which are incomplete or late will be returned to the sender. Where the numbers opting for a particular centre are greater than the accommodation available, the right is reserved to direct candidates to overflow centres in the vicinity.

10. The fees payable in connection with the professional examinations are as follows:

Part I Examination	£6 0s.
For each paper taken separately (upon reference or as a result of exemption in respect of success in an earlier syllabus)	£1 10s.
Exemption from the Part I Examination	£2 10s.
Part II Examination per paper except B21	£1 10s.
Part II, B21 (two papers)	£3 0s.
Exemption from the Part II Examination	£2 10s.

---

[1] In any certificate, a subject taken at different levels only counts once. Where the regulations governing the general education certificate permit the cumulating of passes (as in the G.C.E.), they need not all be obtained at one sitting or from the same examining board.

[2] Overseas certificates are considered in relation (*a*) to the Cambridge Overseas School Certificate, in which a Credit is equated with a Pass at " O " level in the G.C.E., and (*b*) to the Cambridge Higher School Certificate in which a pass at Principal standard is equated with a pass at " A " level in the G.C.E.

* *See special note on p.3 re Post-Graduate syllabus.*

A member will not be required to pay exemption fees in respect of more than one examination. Fees are not refundable to candidates who do not sit an examination. In cases of illness candidates may, on presentation of a satisfactory medical certificate, have the fee carried forward for examination at a later date. In such case a fee voucher will be issued, which must be submitted in lieu of cash with a fresh application in accordance with Regulation 9.

11. The Part I Examination must be taken and passed at one sitting, except that, subject to the rules governing the conduct of the examinations, reference may be allowed. In such case the paper in which reference is given must be taken and passed on the next occasion that the examination is held. A candidate who fails after reference fails the examination, and will have to take all papers again at the next attempt.

The papers in the Part II Examination may be taken together or separately in any order.

12. Candidates who have passed part or parts of former examination syllabuses and are required to complete the Part I Examination must do so before proceeding to the Part II Examination. All outstanding parts of the Part I Examination must be sat and passed at one sitting.[1]

13. The following rules will be observed in sitting the examinations:[2]

(*a*) Smoking is not allowed in the examination room.

(*b*) A candidate leaving the room during the examination (except by special permission and escorted) will not be allowed to return.

(*c*) All books (other than permitted works in Final B13), handbags and cases must be put in charge of the invigilator, and access to them will not be permitted during the examination.

(*d*) A candidate sitting paper 13 from list B of the Part II Examination is permitted the use of certain prescribed works which he must provide for himself (see Syllabus).

(*e*) The Invigilator is not allowed to answer any questions relating to the examination papers.

(*f*) A candidate must write his examination number (which appears on his entry ticket) in the space provided on the front cover of the script book.

(*g*) A candidate must write legibly on both sides of the paper. Both margins must be left. Each answer must begin on a fresh page, the number of the question being written at the top. If an answer is continued on another page, the number of the question must be written at the top of the new page also.

(*h*) A candidate must not write on any part of the script book his name or any means of identifying him other than his official examination number.

(*i*) Supplementary sheets of paper will be supplied on request, and the candidate must write his examination number at the top of each of those used.

(*j*) No part of the script book must be torn out.

---

[1] A list of exemptions and a table of effects follow these regulations.
[2] These are printed on the examination entry ticket.

(*k*) When a candidate has finished his examination he must fasten at the end of the script book any extra sheets, and then seal the script book before handing it to the Invigilator.

14. A candidate who introduces notes, copies another's work, or in the opinion of the Invigilator otherwise behaves improperly will be disqualified and may be excluded from future examinations.

15. The results of his examinations will be sent to each candidate and the lists of successful candidates will be published in the *Library Association Record* for March and September. The names of the successful candidates will be arranged in three classes: Honours, Merit and Pass. No further details beyond those in the official notification can be given to a candidate and no correspondence can be entered into regarding individual cases.

16. A member who wishes to be elected to the Register of Chartered Librarians and who meets the requirements set out in Regulation 1 (above) must apply upon the prescribed form, obtainable from the Secretary, for registration as an Associate. The registration fee of £4 must accompany the application. Those registered may describe themselves as Chartered Librarians and are entitled to use the designation A.L.A.

List of Exemptions

(i) Graduates holding degrees recognized by British Universities.

Exemption from the Part I Examination.

(ii) For having passed Group A of the Registration Examination.

Exemption from Part I, Paper 3, and two of Papers 11, 12, 13 of Part II, List B.

(iii) For having passed Group B of the Registration Examination.

Exemption from Part I, Paper 4, and Paper 21 of Part II, List B.

(iv) For having passed Group C of the Registration Examination.

Exemption from Part I, Papers 1 and 2, and from Part II, List A.

(v) For having passed Group D of the Registration Examination.

Exemption from one of the Papers of Part II, List C.

(vi) For having passed any Part or Parts of the present Final Examination by the date of implementation of the new Syllabus.

No exemption. The 1950 Final Examination will continue to be held up to and including 1968 to enable candidates who at 31st December, 1963, had passed part or parts of the 1950 Final Examination to complete under the old regulations. No further examination under the 1950 regulations will be held thereafter. Alternatively, it will be open to such members to comply with the new requirements for Fellowship.

(vii) For having passed the Part I Diploma Examination of the University of London, or the equivalent examination of Sheffield University, or of Queen's University, Belfast.

Exemption from the Part II Examination.

EXEMPTIONS : TABLE OF EFFECTS

If a candidate had passed Registration Groups :	He would be required to sit the following :
A	Part I : Papers 1, 2 and 4. Part II : One Paper from List A. One Paper from List C. Two other Papers from List B and/or List C, but not B 11, 12 or 13.
A and B	Part I : Papers 1 and 2. Part II : One Paper from List A. One Paper from List C.
A and C	Part I : Paper 4. Part II : One Paper from List C. Two other Papers from List B and/or List C, but not B 11, 12 or 13.
A, B and C	Part II : One Paper from List C.
A and D	Part I : Papers 1, 2 and 4. Part II : One Paper from List A. Two other Papers from List B and/or List C, but not B 11, 12 or 13.
A, C and D	Part I : Paper 4. Part II : Any two Papers from List B and/or List C, but not B 11, 12 or 13.
A, B and D	Part I : Papers 1 and 2. Part II : One Paper from List A.
B	Part I : Papers 1, 2 and 3. Part II : One Paper from List A. One Paper from List C. Two other Papers from List B and/or List C, but not B 21.
B and C	Part I : Paper 3. Part II : One Paper from List C. Two other Papers from List B and/or List C, but not B 21.

If a candidate had passed Registration Groups :	*He would be required to sit the following:*
B *and* D	Part I : Papers 1, 2 and 3. Part II : One Paper from List A. Two other Papers from List B and/or Lits C, but not B 21.
B, C *and* D	Part I : Paper 3. Part II : Any two Papers from List B and/or List C, but not B 21.
C	Part I : Papers 3 and 4. Part II : One Paper from List C. One Paper from List B. Three other Papers from List B and/or List C.
C *and* D	Part I : Papers 3 and 4. Part II: One Paper from List B. Three other Papers from List B and/or List C.
D	Part I : All Papers. Part II : One Paper from List A. One Paper from List B. Three other Papers from List B and/or List C.

SYLLABUS OF PROFESSIONAL EXAMINATIONS

SUMMARY

The Syllabus consists of two Examinations, named the Part I and Part II Examination respectively. The Part I Examination consists of the following four papers of three hours each, all to be taken at one and the same sitting :

1. The Library and the community.
2. Government and control of libraries.
3. The Organization of knowledge.
4. Bibliographical control and service.

The minimum requirement for passing the Part II Examination is six Papers of three hours each, which may be taken together or separately, and in any order. The Papers will be selected by the candidate from three Lists (lettered A, B and C) as follows : one, and only one Paper, from List A, and one or more Papers from each of Lists B and C. Paper B21 will be of six hours duration, broken into two sections for convenience : pass or fail will be in this Paper as a whole, and success in it will count as success in two papers. A candidate may take more than the minimum number of Papers. The lists are set out below.

List A

1. Academic and legal deposit libraries.
2. Special libraries and information bureaux.
3. Public (municipal and county) libraries.

List B

11. Theory of classification.
12. Theory of cataloguing.
13. Practical classification and cataloguing.
21. Bibliography.
22. History of libraries and librarianship.
31. Handling and dissemination of information.
32. Library service for young people in schools and public libraries.
33. Hospital libraries.
91. Archive administration and records management.
92. Palaeography and diplomatic.

List C

The inter-relationships between the subjects of many of the papers in List C are such that entirely clear-cut boundaries cannot always be drawn. However, any single paper will include only such aspects of other subject fields as are essential for the full appreciation of its main subject.

101. Bibliography and librarianship of Old and Middle English, to 1400.
102. —— of English Literature, 1400-1800.
103. —— of Literature in English, 1750 to date.
106. —— of Literature for children.

108.   Bibliography and librarianship of Welsh language and literature.
109.   — — of French language and literature.
110.   — — of Spanish language and literature.
111.   — — of Italian language and literature.
112.   — — of German language and literature.
113.   — — of General and Indo-European philology.
114.   — — of Classics (i.e. Greek and Latin language and literature).
115.   — — of Russian language and literature.
201.   — — of Archaeology and ancient history.
202.   — — of Medieval and modern history.
203.   — — of Geography.
301.   — — of Religion.
302.   — — of Philosophy (including ethics and logic).
303.   — — of Education.
304.   — — of Sociology.
305.   — — of Political science and law.
306.   — — of Economics.
401.   — — of Fine Arts (excluding Music).
402.   — — of Music.
501.   — — of Mechanical engineering.
502.   — — of Civil engineering, building and mining engineering.
503.   — — of Electrical engineering.
504.   — — of History of Science and technology, 1600 to date.
505.   — — of Chemistry and chemical technology.
506.   — — of Natural history and biological sciences.
507.   — — of Medicine.
601.   — — of Africa (South of the Sahara).
602.   — — of the Near East (including Egypt, North Africa and the Sahara).
603.   — — of South Asia (India, Pakistan, Burma, mainland of S.E. Asia, and Indonesia).
604.   — — of the Far East (including Asiatic Russia, China, Japan, and Korea).
605.   — — of the Caribbean Region (including West Indian islands of the Caribbean Sea, the Guianas, and British Honduras).

Other papers may be added from time to time.

DETAILED SYLLABUS

Definitions

Throughout this Syllabus the following definitions apply :

Academic libraries—The Libraries of universities, university colleges, and all other institutions forming parts of, or associated with, universities and other institutions of higher education which have students.

Public libraries   —Rate-supported libraries, whether Municipal or County, open to the general public.

Special libraries   —All libraries which are not academic, public, or national libraries.

Library materials   —Books, periodicals, pamphlets, reports, micro-forms, maps, gramophone records, tapes and all other audio-visual records.

Annotations

The Syllabus is set out in the left-hand column below.   On the right-hand side will be found a column headed " Annotations ".   These constitute a gloss on those parts of the Syllabus which the various Study Groups found to require elucidation, limitation or definition.   The Syllabus is stated in broad terms with the intention of achieving a maximum life : the Annotations are an interpretation in the light of current knowledge and conditions, and they will be amended by the Board of Assessors on the advice of Study Groups from time to time.   Such amendments will appear in the L.A. RECORD and in subsequent editions of the *Students' handbook* and *Syllabus of examinations,* etc.

PART I EXAMINATION

Syllabus

Annotations

Questions set in the Part I Examination will normally relate to British practice predominantly.

Paper 1.   *The Library and the community* (compulsory 3-hour paper)

The general aim of this Paper is to put the library into its social context, showing the growing needs for it and how it attempts to meet those needs.

History of libraries and librarianship in the British Isles during the nineteenth and twentieth centuries.

The library in society, its aims and functions.   The kinds of libraries and the services appropriate to different kinds of libraries : national, academic, public and special.

The social function of the library — relationship of libraries to other media of communication and major influences in society, e.g. education, use of leisure, censorship, provision for research. Some comparisons with other countries are desirable.

Library co-operation in all its aspects.

National, regional, local schemes of stock-building, service, interlending, storage. Schemes within subject groups, e.g. education, medicine, engineering.   International exchange and loan. Comparison with significant schemes of co-operation in other countries.

Professional and other associations connected with librarianship.

No more is required here than a knowledge of the functions of the various societies, such as The Library Association, Aslib, National Book League, the bibliographical societies, the British Council, I.F.L.A., F.I.D., Unesco, and their contributions to the community.

Paper 2.   *Government and control of Libraries* (compulsory 3-hour paper)

The aim of this Paper is to deal with the practical conduct of the institutions which have evolved as the result of the considerations covered by Paper 1.

Syllabus	*Annotations*
Government, management and finance of libraries. Staffing and division of work.	*Questions will be set on the general principles involved and may require illustration by the practice in particular kinds of libraries.*
	Government includes the body responsible for the control of the library and any relevant legislative provisions.
	Management includes both principles and methods of library administration.
	Finance includes all aspects of the source and control of income and expenditure.
	Staffing includes the principles of personnel management : staff establishments : professional and non-professional duties : recruitment, and in-service training.
Stock-control ; selection ; order and accession methods of library material ; maintenance of stock. Administration and facilities of, and admission to, the departments of libraries.	*The bibliographical aspects of book selection are dealt with in Paper 4.*

Paper 3. The Organization of knowledge (compulsory 3-hour paper)

The organization of knowledge through classification schemes, catalogues and indexes. A knowledge of the basic principles of classification and the structure and main features of general schemes of classification.	*This section does not relate to any one kind of library, but is to provide the basis for all kinds of library workers. The aim is to ensure that every librarian is familiar with the form and with the general features of the Bibliographic, Colon, Decimal, Library of Congress, Subject and Universal Decimal classification schemes. It would not involve questions of comparative treatment of subjects. Questions involving practical work may be set and candidates will need to have done as much practical work as is necessary to understand and use catalogues properly.*
Author and title cataloguing : a general comparative knowledge of the A.A., A.L.A., and B.M. Codes.	*This involves an understanding of the purposes of the codes, and the main underlying principles of each group of rules. A knowledge of individual rules will only be required to exemplify principles.*
Descriptive cataloguing.	*Simplified and selective cataloguing : short, standard, and full entries and where they are used. Note that catalogue entries can refer to periodicals, music, gramophone records and other materials besides books.*
Subject cataloguing. Types of entry : contents and purposes.	*This brings out the difference between subject-indexing and subject entry. Chain procedure and subject lists.*
Physical forms and forms of arrangement of catalogues and indexes. Filing rules.	*This includes subject indexes to information and periodicals.*

4B

Syllabus	*Annotations*
Centralized and co-operative cataloguing and indexing.	*L. of C. and B.N.B. catalogues and cards. Local co-operative production of cards, and of indexes.*

Paper 4.   Bibliographical control and service (compulsory 3 hour paper)

General bibliographical control.	*Bibliographical control is the development and maintenance of a system of adequate recording of all forms of material, published or unpublished, printed, audio-visual, or otherwise, which add to the sum of human knowledge and information. Brief historical background, present problems and some solutions (e.g. Unesco, national bibliographic centres, regional activity) ; universal bibliographies ; national bibliography of the U.K.*
Selection of library materials : aids and guides to stock building.	*Covers only aids and guides to stock building. (Social factors come in Paper 1. Administrative aspects come in Paper 2. Full treatment in relation to special subjects come in Part II List C papers.)*
Bibliographical service : enquiry techniques, assessment of enquiries, literature surveys and searches, preparation of bibliographies, bulletins, abstracts and indexes. Methods of bibliographic citation.	
Types of reference material and their uses.	*e.g. dictionaries, encyclopaedias, year books, directories, atlases, maps, periodicals (including abstracting and indexing services), statistical material, biographical materials, audio-visual materials, " unpublished " materials. Includes publishing by H.M.S.O. and international organizations.*
Contemporary book and periodical production ; re-binding ; the uses of documentary reproduction including relevant copyright problems. Micro-form publishing.	*A general outline of the processes which go to the production of books, periodicals, etc., from the delivery of the MS.: from the librarian's viewpoint not the publisher's or technician's.*

PART II EXAMINATION
List A, Papers 1-3

Apart from the first paragraph of the Syllabus of each Paper, the Papers in List A are concerned primarily with British practice, although candidates are expected to have some knowledge of relevant developments abroad which are making significant contributions of international interest.   This implies that candidates will be expected to have paid some attention to important work done outside the British Isles, and to reveal this in their answers where appropriate.   Apart from questions on the first section of each Paper, however, there will be none on overseas developments as such, without an alternative within the same question.

Syllabus	*Annotations*

List A, Paper 1.   *Academic and legal deposit libraries* (3-hour paper)

The history and functions of Academic and legal deposit libraries, with special reference to those in the United Kingdom, the Commonwealth, Europe, and the United States of America.

" Europe " here means those European countries in which the libraries covered possess features of special interest to British students ; e.g. Scandinavian countries, France, Germany, Holland, U.S.S.R.

Government ;   finance ;   organization ; administration.

Buildings : siting, planning, equipment and fittings.

Outline requirements for the guidance of architects and supplies officers, who will do the work, not detailed specification. Includes both (1) heating, ventilating, lighting, etc., equipment and fittings, and (2) library equipment and fittings.

Staff : selection, training and qualifications, salaries and conditions, duties and deployment.

Stock : administrative aspects of selection and acquisition, and of classification and cataloguing, access and control.

Special departments and collections ; departmental libraries.

Administrative aspects of technical departments (e.g. a bindery).

Relation to teaching and research : instruction of students :   services to outside readers :   regulations.

Academic and legal deposit libraries and co-operation.

List A, Paper 2.   *Special libraries and information bureaux* (3-hour paper)

The history and functions of special libraries, information bureaux, and those national libraries that have a specialized function (including the N.C.L.) with emphasis on those in the United Kingdom, the Commonwealth, Europe and the United States of America.

" Europe " here means those European countries in which the libraries covered possess features of special interest to British students : e.g. Scandinavian countries, France, Germany, Holland, U.S.S.R.

Main features of organization, function and administration, with special reference to variations in type of library according to specialization of subject and clientele.

Building : siting, planning, equipment, and fittings.

Outline requirements for the guidance of architects and supplies officers, who will do the work, not detailed specification. Includes both (1) heating, ventilating, lighting, etc., equipment and fittings, and (2) library equipment and fittings.

Staff : selection, training and qualifications, salaries and conditions, duties and deployment.

Stock : administrative aspects of selection and acquisition ;   of classification, cataloguing and indexing ;   and of the handling of unpublished material, including confidential documents.

With particular reference to such material as periodicals, pamphlets, reports, correspondence, press cuttings, trade literature, etc. Precautions in indexing, handling, etc., of unpublished material.

Special libraries and co-operation.

Syllabus   *Annotations*

List A, Paper 3.   Public (*municipal and county*) *libraries* (3-hour paper)

History, development and characteristics of rate-supported libraries in the United Kingdom. Comparative study of public library provision in the Commonwealth, Europe and the United States of America.

Includes standards of service and proposals for future development. " Europe " here means those European countries in which the public library service possesses features of special interest to British students ; e.g. Scandinavian countries, France, Germany, Holland, U.S.S.R.

Library law and other relevant legislation in the United Kingdom ; byelaws and regulations.

The emphasis will be on those aspects of law which the Municipal or County Librarian will need to know in the course of his duty. It will not include those aspects of Library Law and Common Law which would normally be outside the province of a practising Librarian. This means, on the one hand, that it would not be unreasonable to expect a working knowledge of the simpler basic definitions within the framework of common law. i.e. What is theft? What is assault? On the other hand, it would not be reasonable to expect detailed knowledge of the legal aspects of compulsory purchase, although the powers are detailed in the 1919 Act, Section 6, and have been since amended by the Local Government Act, 1933 and various other statutes. Within these two limits candidates would be expected to have a clear understanding of the law concerning more conventional Library matters such as Bye-laws, Committees, charges for admission, fines, the appointment and dismissal of staff.

Government ; finance ; organization ; administration.

Includes committee work : the organization of library departments including binderies, photographic departments, etc.: lending services, reference services, subject departments, special services, junior services, and in county libraries, organization of H.Q., urban, rural and special services : branch organization, regional organization. " Special services " includes service to prisoners, handicapped persons, etc.

Buildings : siting, planning, equipment, and fittings.

Outline requirements for the guidance of architects and supplies officers, who will do the work, not detailed specification. Includes both (1) heating, ventilating, lighting, etc., equipment and fittings, and (2) library equipment and fittings.

Staff : selection, training and qualifications, salaries and conditions, duties and deployment.

Stock : administrative aspects of selection and acquisition ; classification and cataloguing ; access and control.

Public libraries and co-operation.

List B, Paper 11.   Theory of classification (3-hour paper)

Historical development of the theory of library classification, with special reference to the period since 1876.

Library classification means here the schemes of classification for libraries as well as classification as practised in libraries, for the organization of library materials.

Syllabus	*Annotations*
Comparative study of major general schemes of classification, their development and principles, and their application in general and special libraries.	*At present this means the following classification schemes ; Decimal, U.D.C., Bibliographic, Library of Congress, Colon and Subject.*
Construction, revision and modification of general schemes and of schemes for special collections and for particular purposes.	
Notation.	
Relation of classification to methods of information storage and retrieval, including mechanical and electronic methods.	
Relation of classification to subject cataloguing and indexing.	

List B, Paper 12.   *Theory of cataloguing* (3-hour paper)

	This paper deals with the listing and description of library materials for the purpose of catalogues, bibliographies, indexes, abstracts, etc.
History and purposes of cataloguing.	*The purposes of catalogues have been different at different times in the history of cataloguing and have led to the development of different types of catalogue (e.g. incunabula, short-title, subject catalogues).*
Comparative study of the major cataloguing codes, including their development and revision.	*At present this means the British Museum, Anglo-American, American Library Association (1949), Library of Congress, Cutter and Vatican Library Codes, and the Prussian Instructions.*
Application of the principles of cataloguing to general and special problems.	*The special problems include periodicals, corporate authors with complicated histories, and analytical entries.*
Theory and practice in dictionary, classified and name catalogues, subject headings and subject indexing.	
Problems arising from the different physical forms of catalogues.	
Relation of cataloguing to methods of information storage and retrieval, including mechanical and electronic methods.	

List B, Paper 13.   *Practical classification and cataloguing* (3-hour paper)

This paper is intended to test general competence in practical cataloguing and classifying. Candidates will be given a number of facsimiles or transcripts of title-pages (with informative notes) which will form the basis of tests in classification, descriptive cataloguing, and selection of headings for main and added entries and	*The examples set may include periodicals and other serials. All examples will be in English. Generally speaking candidates will be expected to produce subject headings which conform to English terminology, even when they use a list of subject headings of American origin (e.g. " railways " not " railroads ").*

Syllabus | *Annotations*

references. They will be permitted the choice of one of the following general schemes of classification : Bibliographic, Colon, Decimal, Library of Congress, Subject, U.D.C. Each will be required to provide for his own use a copy of the scheme in which he chooses to be examined ; and will also be permitted to take into the examination a copy of the Anglo-American code, and of either Sears' *List of subject headings,* or, Library of Congress *Subject headings used in the dictionary catalogue.*

List B, Paper 21.   *Bibliography* (6-hour paper divided into two, to be taken at one and the same attempt.)

Predecessors and early forms of the book, their materials and make-up.

Background knowledge sufficient to enable comparisons to be made with the nature and characteristics of printed books.

History of printing and the evolution of the book.

After the introduction into Europe of printing from movable type, " History of printing " is limited to Western Europe, the United States and the Commonwealth.

Printing materials and methods. The materials of which books have been and are now being made.

Excluding " near-print " and " office-printing ".

History and methods of binding and binding decoration.

Principles of binding techniques, and outline knowledge of main developments in binding and decorative styles.

The functions and methods of book illustration from the decoration of manuscripts to the present day.

Book design ; fine printing ; private presses.

The function of analytical and descriptive bibliography. The development of bibliographical method, investigation and research. Principles of collation and bibliographical description. Principles of bibliographical editing.

Standards based upon such works as Fredson Bowers, McKerrow and the work and publications of the bibliographical societies and institutions.

History and present state of authorship, publishing and bookselling (including institutional and non-trade publications). Book trade bibliography.

This section is confined to Great Britain except for those events abroad directly affecting British practices.

List B, Paper 22.   *History of libraries and librarianship* (3-hour paper)

Classical and medieval libraries in broad outline only. The dissolution of the monasteries and the development of academic and national libraries, mainly in Great Britain but in broad outline for Europe also. Growth of the great private collections from Cotton onwards. Naudé ; Leibniz. The development of municipal and parish libraries, especially in Great Britain. The Royal Society ; scientific and learned society libraries.

This paper is concerned mainly with the development of libraries of all types from the sixteenth century to the present day, with special reference to Great Britain. Some familiarity with the earlier background, and with the main trends of development in Europe and elsewhere will, however, be expected.

Syllabus	*Annotations*

Circulating and subscription libraries.
Mechanics' Institute libraries.
The broad lines of the development of the modern libraries and of national library services in all parts of the world, and their social background.

List B, Paper 31.   *Handling and dissemination of information* (3-hour paper)

The means by which information may be disseminated from special libraries. Methods of preparation and reproduction of the publications of Library and Information Departments. Copyright in dissemination. The language barrier in dissemination. Abstracting and the form and use of abstract journals. Finding and meeting users' needs. Principles and practice of indexing in special libraries. Theory of information retrieval. Mechanical and electronic methods for processing and retrieval of information.

The emphasis in this paper will be on the usual operations of a Library and Information Unit. The handling and processing of material must be considered with a view to the most efficient dissemination of the information it contains. Consideration of the language barrier includes co-operation in translation, and cover-to-cover work.

List B, Paper 32.   *Library service for young people in schools and public libraries* (3-hour paper)

Candidates for this paper are strongly advised to offer at the same time paper C106, as there is considerable material which forms a common background to both papers.

Library services for children and young people to the age of 18.

History, development and characteristics of public and school libraries in the United Kingdom, and overseas where significant.

Includes social, educational and historical reasons for development, and aims and purpose.

General provisions of current educational legislation relevant to libraries.

Sufficient to provide background of understanding for school library work in the United Kingdom : e.g. the kinds of schools and who provides them.

Main features of organization, function and administration of libraries for young people.

Including reference to the various agencies concerned, such as local education authorities, public libraries, voluntary organizations.

Buildings : siting, planning, equipment and fittings.

Outline requirements for the guidance of architects and supplies officers, who will do the work, not detailed specification. Includes both (1) heating, ventilating, lighting, etc., equipment and fittings, and (2) library equipment and fittings.

Staff : selection, training and qualifications, salaries and conditions, duties and deployment.

Mental growth of children and adolescents, linguistic and reading ability at various ages, social development, backward children.

Relevant to library services and book provision. Includes the development of children and adolescents.

List B, Paper 33.   *Hospital libraries* (3-hour paper)

This paper deals with the provision of a general library service to hospital patients and staff in all kinds of hospitals, and not with medical librarianship as such.

Syllabus	*Annotations*
The history and functions of the hospital library in the United Kingdom, and overseas where significant. Types of hospital library organization.	*Deals with hospital libraries provided by any agency, including the hospital itself, and with both complete and partial services.*
Main features of hospital organization, function, and administration.	*Sufficient to provide the background of understanding for the carrying out of hospital library work.*
Government ; finance ; organization ; administration.	
Buildings : siting, planning, equipment and fittings.	*Outline requirements for the guidance of architects and supplies officers, who will do the work, not detailed specification. Includes both (1) heating, ventilating, lighting, etc., equipment and fittings, and (2) library equipment and fittings.*
Staff : selection, training and qualifications, salaries and conditions, duties and deployment.	*This includes both paid and unpaid staff.*
Stock : administrative aspects of selection and acquisition ; care and maintenance ; classification and cataloguing ; access and control.	*Any special precautions in handling, etc., come here.*
Hospital libraries and co-operation.	
The psychology of the sick : general principles of mental and physical rehabilitation. The therapeutic value of reading. Extension work with patients.	

List B, Paper 91. *Archive administration and records management* (3-hour paper)

The provision made for the preservation and use of archives and records in the United Kingdom.	*Covers archives and records of central and local government, public corporations, ecclesiastical bodies, business concerns, private and public schools, societies and associations, etc.: estate, family and private archives.*
Definition of archives. *Respect des fonds.* Provenance and location of British archive accumulations.	*Archive quality, the archive group, distinction between archival and non-archival material.*
Functions and duties of archivists and keepers of records.	*Includes relations with other services such as public library, record offices, etc.*
Organization and administration of record Offices and Archive Departments.	*Includes an outline knowledge of Public Record Office and County Record Offices.*
Building : siting, planning, equipment, fittings.	
Acquisition : gifts, deposits, purchases : classification: cataloguing: calendaring, indexing, publication, guides, photography and photocopying.	
Accessibility : publications, guides, extension work.	*Includes search room, rules and regulations, etc. Lectures, exhibitions, educational activities, co-operation.*
Physical care of archives : storage : repair : binding.	
Staff : selection, training and qualifications, salaries and conditions of service, duties and deployment.	

Syllabus	*Annotations*
Records Management : appraisal and selection : problems arising from modern record media.	*Includes use of microfilm, tapes, etc.*
Organizations associated with preservation and administration of archives.	
History of archive preservation.	

List B, Paper 92. *Palaeography and diplomatic* (3-hour paper)

Handwriting of Western Europe, with special reference to English administrative hands. Development of individual letter forms. Abbreviations, punctuation, numerals, etc.	*Includes transcription of Latin and English documents and translation from Latin into English.*
Diplomatic : influence of administration and other factors on documentary form : reliability of archives as source material : forgery.	
Materials used for writing : paper, parchment, vellum, wood, pens, ink, etc. Illuminations : scriptoria.	
Scribes, notaries, scriveners, writing-masters.	
Chronology.	
Seals : purpose methods of attachment, repair, etc.	
Description of classes of documents.	
Editing of documents.	
Bibliography.	

List C, Papers 101-605. *Bibliography and librarianship in a special subject field* (3-hour paper)

	The inter-relationships between the subjects of many of the papers in List C are such that entirely clear-cut boundaries cannot always be drawn. However, any single paper will include only such aspects of other subject fields as are essential for the full appreciation of its main subject. The examination will concern itself with the bibliography and librarianship of the subject, and will not seek to test subject knowledge as such. Candidates will be assumed to possess a sufficient background knowledge of the subject to enable them to grasp the bibliography of the subject. It is recognized that each of the sections of this Syllabus will not apply equally to all subjects. Papers set will reflect the varying emphasis given to parts of this Syllabus in different subjects.
Bibliographical apparatus : bibliographies, catalogues, abstracts, reference works. Principal works and editions.	
Special types of materials.	*e.g. Festschriften, Handbücher, theses, periodicals, reviews of progress, catalogues of specimens, log-books, maps, tables, sound recordings.*

Syllabus	*Annotations*
Classification and cataloguing : treatment of the subject in general bibliographical classification schemes : special schemes of classification : special problems of classification and cataloguing within the subject field.	
Outstanding collections in the field, their contents, special features and availability.	*Includes guides to libraries.*
Societies and bibliographical and other organizations in the field, and their publications.	
Selection of material. Exploitation of the collection.	*Selection of materials includes policy of selection as determined by clientele and co-operative provision. Exploitation includes assistance to readers, display and storage.*
Production of bibliographical aids.	

The above is the general syllabus applying to all the following papers. Any special annotations will follow the list of papers.

101. Bibliography and librarianship of Old and Middle English, to 1400.
102. — — of English literature, 1400-1800.
103. — — of Literature in English, 1750 to date.
106. — — of Literature for children.
108. — — of Welsh language and literature.
109. — — of French language and literature.
110. — — of Spanish language and literature.
111. — — of Italian language and literature.
112. — — of German language and literature.
113. — — of General and Indo-European philology.
114. — — of Classics (i.e. Greek and Latin language and literature).
115. — — of Russian language and literature.
201. — — of Archaeology and ancient history.
202. — — of Medieval and modern history.
203. — — of Geography.
301. — — of Religion.
302. — — of Philosophy (including ethics and logic).
303. — — of Education.
304. — — of Sociology (i.e. sociological theory, social psychology, social anthropology, social statistics, social surveys, social services, social welfare, demography, modern social history since 1760).
305. — — of Political science and law (i.e. political theory, international relations, current political affairs, public administration, law of Common Law countries, and international and comparative law).
306. — — of Economics (i.e. economic theory, economic statistics, financial, industrial and commercial organization, including business management, world economic and commercial history since 1760, and current economic conditions, international economic activity).
401. — — of Fine Arts (excluding Music).
402. — — of Music.

501. — — of Mechanical engineering.

502. — — of Civil engineering, building and mining engineering.

503. — — of Electrical engineering.

504. — — of History of Science and technology, 1600 to date.

505. — — of Chemistry and chemical technology.

506. — — of Natural history and biological sciences.

507. — — of Medicine.

601. — — of Africa (South of the Sahara).

602. — — of the Near East (including Egypt, North Africa and the Sahara).

603. — — of South Asia (India, Pakistan, Burma, mainland of S.E. Asia, and Indonesia).

604. — — of the Far East (including Asiatic Russia, China, Japan, and Korea).

605. — — of the Caribbean Region (including W. Indian islands of the Caribbean Sea, the Guianas and Br. Honduras).

Special Annotations relating to individual Papers in List C.

List C, Paper 101. *Bibliography and librarianship of Old and Middle English, to* 1400.

List C, Paper 102. *Bibliography and librarianship of English literature,* 1400-1800.

List C, Paper 103. *Bibliography and librarianship of Literature in English,* 1750 *to date.*

The questions set for these papers will either be general, or in such form as to permit a candidate to cite his own author or exemplify from his own period ; or, where a particular author is named, will provide alternatives within the question by naming authors of similar importance in other recognized periods of English literary history.

" Outstanding collections " includes collections situated overseas (e.g. Folger Shakespeare Library, or the Boswell papers at Yale).

Periodicals will include American ones (e.g. P.M.L.A. or Hudson review).

List C, Paper 106. *Bibliography and librarianship of Literature for Children.*

Candidates for this paper are strongly advised to offer at the same time paper B32, as there is considerable material which forms a common background to both papers.

Library services for children and young people to the age of 18.

" Bibliographical apparatus . . ." refers to British sources in detail : important Commonwealth and American sources in outline.

" Principal works and editions " refers to literature for children published in the United Kingdom (to include significant Commonwealth, U.S.A. and translated publications). Includes criteria for assessing different types of children's literature, with significant examples. Questions will be asked expecting detailed knowledge of certain fields of children's literature, both fiction and non-fiction, the choice of these fields being left to the candidate.

" Societies . . ." includes principal international and foreign organizations ; principal awards in children's literature.

List C, Paper 108. *Bibliography and librarianship of Welsh language and literature.*

Questions may be answered in either English or Welsh at the discretion of the candidate.

List C, Paper 201. *Bibliography and librarianship of Archaeology and ancient history.*

Covers prehistoric archaeology, European and classical archaeology and the Barbarian invasions, Western Asiatic archaeology and history to the Arab invasions.

List C, Paper 202. *Bibliography and librarianship of Medieval and modern history.*
Covers medieval and modern history of the British Isles from the Barbarian invasions, including the
auxiliary sciences (e.g. biography, genealogy, heraldry, numismatics).

List C, Paper 401. *Bibliography and librarianship of the Fine arts (excluding
music).*
The scope of this paper comprises class 700 in the Decimal Classification, excluding photography,
cinema and recreations, but including costume and theatre arts (i.e. stage design).

List C, Paper 502. *Bibliography and librarianship of Civil engineering, building
and mining engineering.*
Covers municipal, sanitary, mining and structural engineering, building technology, relevant aspects of
nuclear engineering, town and country planning, traffic engineering.

List C, Paper 503. *Bibliography and librarianship of Electrical engineering.*
Covers generation, transmission, distribution and utilization of electric power ; instruments and
instrumentation ; applied magnetism ; applied electrostatics ; electric lighting ; electric traction ;
electrochemistry ; thermo-electricity and electroheating ; electromagnetic waves and oscillations ;
electronics ; telecommunications ; electric welding ; automation and control ; computors ; nuclear power ;
materials.
It includes theory and practice ; economics and statistics ; mathematical and physical sciences ; and
mechanical engineering and metallurgy so far as these subjects are necessary to coverage of the main field.

List C, Paper 504. *Bibliography and librarianship of History of Science and
technology, 1600 to date.*
To cover both science and technology, and to be extended to include 20th century.

List C, Paper 505. *Bibliography and librarianship of Chemistry and Chemical
technology.*
Covers pure chemistry ; chemical engineering ; biochemistry, crystallography, and the chief chemical
industries : dyestuffs, fine and heavy chemicals, petro-chemicals and coal derivatives, Industrial micro-
biology, food and drugs, plastics and paint.

List C, Paper 506. *Bibliography and librarianship of Natural history and biological sciences.*
Covers geology and descriptive mineralogy, including palaeontology ; and biology including genetics,
cytology, ecology, botany, zoology, bacteriology, mycology and parasitology.

List C, Paper 605. *Bibliography and librarianship of the Caribbean Region.*
For the purposes of this examination the Caribbean comprises the West Indian islands of the Caribbean
Sea, the Guianas and British Honduras. The wider Caribbean area (including the Bahamas, Central
America and the Spanish Main) will also be included, but only in so far as the bibliography and librarian-
ship of these areas have any direct bearing on or relationship to those of the area defined above. The
Syllabus is principally concerned with English-speaking territories of the Caribbean, but the bibliography
of the non-English-speaking countries is not excluded.

Entrance Examination

PREFATORY NOTE

It is the intention of the Council that in due course recruitment to the
profession shall be entirely from graduates and from candidates who have
successfully completed a two-year sixth-form course at a good standard,
with at least two passes at " A " level in the General Certificate of Education
(see Professional Examinations Regulation 4).   Until the end of 1967 the
Council will hold an examination of a standard comparable with " A " level
in the General Certificate of Education in library subjects.   This examination is based on the assumption that candidates for it will be 18 years of
age or more, although no age limit is prescribed, and that they have com-

pleted at least one year's service in a library at the time of sitting the examination, although this is not a condition of entry. This examination is not part of the professional examinations, the first of which is the Part I Examination.

REGULATIONS

1. The Entrance Examination is open only to members of the Library Association.

2. A candidate for the examination must produce evidence that he has obtained a suitable General Certificate of Education, or has passed an acceptable equivalent general examination.[1]

The minimum requirement from holders of the General Certificate of Education (England) are 5 passes at Ordinary level, or 4 passes if one of them be at Advanced level: one of the passes must be in English Language. From holders of the Scottish Certificate of Education the minimum requirements are 5 passes at Ordinary Grade, or 4 passes if one or two be at Higher Grade, one of the passes must be in English. The appropriate certificate for Northern Ireland is the Grammar School Senior Certificate in which a pass is accepted as equivalent to a pass at the corresponding level in the General Certificate of Education. A subject taken at different levels counts only once. The passes need not all be obtained at one sitting.[2]

3. The examination will be held in the Summer and Winter of each year. The dates of examinations will be published in the February and August issues of the *Library Association Record*.

4. Candidates for the examination must apply to the Secretary on the appropriate form on or before March 31st for entrance to the Summer examination, and on or before September 30th for the Winter Examination. A form of entry will be provided upon application. This must be returned, together with the fee, any necessary documents, and two stamped self-addressed envelopes. Applications which are late or incomplete will be returned to the sender.

5. The fee for the Entrance Examination is £2 10s.

6. Fees are not refundable to candidates who do not sit the examination. In cases of illness candidates may, on presentation of a satisfactory medical certificate, have the fee carried forward for an examination at a later date. In such case a fee voucher will be issued, and must be submitted in lieu of cash with a fresh application in accordance with Entrance Examination Regulation 4.

---

[1] Overseas certificates are considered in relation to the Cambridge Overseas School Certificate, in which a Credit is equated with a Pass at Ordinary level in the G.C.E. Cambridge Overseas School Certificates are accepted as follows:

1st Division certificate; 2nd Division certificate providing it contains a Credit in English language; 3rd Division certificate only if it contains five Credits, including one in English language.

[2] Since applicants for registration as Chartered Librarians require a pass in either a language other than English or a science, intending entrants to the profession are urged to ensure that they include one of these in the subjects they take in the Certificate.

7. The examination must be taken and passed at one sitting. It will be marked as a whole and results will be based upon the aggregate marks obtained.

8. The rules set out in Regulation 13 of the professional examinations and printed on the entry tickets, will be observed in sitting the examination.

9. A candidate who introduces notes, copies another's work, or in the opinion of the Invigilator otherwise behaves improperly will be disqualified and may be excluded from future examinations.

10. The result of his examination will be sent to each candidate and the list of successful candidates will be published in the *Library Association Record* for March and September. No further details beyond those in the official notification can be given to a candidate and no correspondence can be entered into regarding individual cases.

SYLLABUS

The Entrance examination consists of four Papers of 1½ hours each, as follows:

(1) LIBRARIANSHIP: PURPOSE   *(One paper of 1½ hours)*

The aims and scope of the library service. The services available in all types of library. Inter-library co-operation. Professional education and qualification. Professional associations.

(2) LIBRARIANSHIP: METHODS   *(One paper of 1½ hours)*

How libraries are governed and financed. Staffing and the division of work. The ordering and receipt, preparation, care and custody of books, periodicals and other related material. The admission and registration of readers. Circulation methods, reservation, inter-lending of material, personal service, publicity.

(3) LIBRARY STOCK: DESCRIPTION AND ARRANGEMENT
(One paper of 1½ hours)

The parts of books and periodicals. Simple bibliographical terms. The practical purposes of classification in libraries. Parts of a classification scheme. Shelf arrangement, guiding and display. The purposes of reading lists. The purposes of cataloguing. The types and forms of catalogue. The details given in catalogue entries. References. The functions of subject headings in a dictionary catalogue and of indexes to a classified catalogue. The arrangement of the catalogue, alphabetizing and filing, guide cards and labels. Centralized cataloguing and the use of the *British national bibliography*.

(4) LIBRARY STOCK: USE   *(One paper of 1½ hours)*

The value and use of the more important types of reference book, e.g. encyclopaedias, year books, directories, dictionaries, indexes to periodicals, abstracts, book-trade lists, books of quotations, biographical reference works, atlases. Abbreviations used in books.

1950 FINAL EXAMINATION

From 1st January, 1964, admission to Fellowship will be by Thesis only, except that any Member who at that date has passed or has been exempted from one or more Parts of the 1950 Final Examination will have the option of completing under the 1950 Syllabus. For this purpose the Council will continue to hold the 1950 Final Examination up to and including Winter 1968, but not thereafter.

This Syllabus is therefore set out below.

1950 Final Examination

This is designed to test the mature judgment of the candidates. Acquaintance with periodical library literature and contemporary development in each field will be expected. The examination is in four parts, each of two 3-hour papers. Parts may be taken together or separately in any order, but both papers of any one Part must be attempted and passed together. There is no reference in the Final Examination.

1. BIBLIOGRAPHY AND BOOK SELECTION

    The main emphasis in the Final Examination is on the practical application to given situations of what has been learned as fact at Registration level.

2. LIBRARY ORGANIZATION AND ADMINISTRATION

    1ST PAPER : GENERAL
    2ND PAPER : One of the following :
    - (a) PUBLIC LIBRARIES
    - (b) UNIVERSITY AND COLLEGE LIBRARIES
    - (c) SPECIAL LIBRARIES AND INFORMATION BUREAUX

3. LITERATURE AND LIBRARIANSHIP OF SPECIAL SUBJECTS : One of the alternatives 3(a) to 3(i) :

    3(a) ENGLISH LITERATURE : One of the following periods :
    - (i) English literature up to 1550
    - (ii) English literature and outstanding foreign literature available in English, 1550-1660
    - (iii) English literature and outstanding foreign literature available in English, 1660-1780
    - (iv) English and American literature and outstanding foreign literature available in English, 1780-1900
    - (v) English literature (including American literature and the literature of the British Commonwealth) and outstanding foreign literature available in English, 1900 onwards

3(b) PHILOSOPHY AND RELIGION

3(c) SOCIAL SCIENCES (INCLUDING COMMERCE AND LAW)

3(d) SCIENCE AND TECHNOLOGY

    1ST PAPER : *General Science*

    2ND PAPER : (i) *Mathematical and physical sciences, pure and applied (excluding chemistry)*

        OR (ii) *Chemistry and chemical technology*

        OR (iii) *Natural history and biological sciences, pure and applied (excluding medicine)*

        OR (iv) *Engineering and building technology*

3(e) FINE ARTS (EXCLUDING MUSIC)

3(f) MUSIC

3(g) MEDICINE

3(h) HISTORY AND ARCHAEOLOGY

3(i) GENERAL AND EUROPEAN PHILOLOGY

4. ONE OF THE FOLLOWING :

    4(a) PALAEOGRAPHY AND ARCHIVES

    4(b) LIBRARY WORK WITH YOUNG PEOPLE

    4(c) ADVANCED CLASSIFICATION AND CATALOGUING

    4(d) HISTORICAL BIBLIOGRAPHY

    4(e) PRESENTATION AND DISSEMINATION OF INFORMATION

    4(f) LITERATURE OF WALES

Final Examination

FINAL, PART 1. BIBLIOGRAPHY AND BOOK SELECTION

(Two papers of 3 hours)

Essentials of book production : e.g. materials and manufacture of paper ; type ; the parts of a book ; hand and machine composition ; ink and press work ; printing reproduction processes and modern methods of documentary reproduction for books, articles, etc.; processes of illustration ; materials and methods of binding.

Collation and description of books. Editions, issues, impressions and reprints.

The sources of bibliographies : e.g. books of reference ; bibliographies of bibliography ; universal, national (including trade) and comprehensive subject and author bibliographies ; official publications ; catalogues of libraries ; lists of and indexes to periodicals.

Methods of compiling and arranging bibliographies, general and selective.

Selection of books and periodicals for libraries of various kinds and sizes.

Outstanding books in important subjects together with standard reference material ; e.g. encyclopaedias, directories, dictionaries, code books, gazetteers, Government and other official publications.

FINAL, PART 2. LIBRARY ORGANIZATION AND ADMINIS-TRATION
(Two papers of 3 hours)

1ST PAPER : GENERAL

Definition, scope and purpose of libraries. The general history and development of libraries in Great Britain. The great libraries of the world. Library co-operation, regional, national, international. Legal deposit. The library profession. Professional education. Professional associations.

2ND PAPER : One of the following :

(a) PUBLIC LIBRARIES. Current legislation in the United Kingdom and the outline of that in the Dominions and the U.S.A. Bye-laws and regulations. Constitution and powers of committees. Finance. Buildings and equipment. Population and other factors in relation to library provision. Architectural competitions. Development, function and methods of library departments including special services. Office routine. Staff : functions, qualifications, training, salaries and conditions. Extension work. Co-operation between library authorities. Future development of libraries in the United Kingdom.

(b) UNIVERSITY AND COLLEGE LIBRARIES. The history, development and characteristics of university libraries in Great Britain, the Dominions and Colonies, Europe and America. Government and finance. Qualifications, duties, training and conditions of service of librarians and staff. Planning and design of buildings and fittings. Administration. Office routine. Rules and regulations. Special departments and collections ; departmental libraries. Routine methods. Book selection and acquisition. Relation to university teaching and research ; instruction of students ; services to outside readers. Access and control.

(c) SPECIAL LIBRARIES AND INFORMATION BUREAUX. The history and development of special libraries in Great Britain, the Dominions and Colonies, Europe and America. The different types of special libraries—government departments, societies, firms, chambers of commerce, trade associations, commercial information services, industrial research organizations, etc. The relations between special libraries and other types of libraries. Finance, administration and staffing. Office routine. Premises—planning, arrangement, equipment and fittings. Book selection. Sources of information. The arrangement and utilization of material—classification, cataloguing, filing, indexing. Statistics and records. The library and the user—distribution of information, routing of periodicals, reference methods, precautions in handling of confidential material. Special services—translations, indexing, reproductions. Treatment of special material—current and fugitive material, maps, plans, pamphlets, periodicals, etc. Abstracts and abstracting.

FINAL, PART 3. LITERATURE AND LIBRARIANSHIP OF SPECIAL SUBJECTS
(Two papers of 3 hours)

One of the alternatives 3(a) to 3(i).

Candidates will be expected to have a general knowledge of the subject and a critical knowledge of the outstanding works in their particular field, including bibliographies, periodicals, reports of learned societies, indexes, etc.; to appreciate the special problems in cataloguing, classification and shelving which the material presents and to have a knowledge of the relevant foreign and English societies and libraries which are associated with the field.

Two papers will be set in each subject. In 3(d) the first paper will cover general science and the second paper special science.

3(a) ENGLISH LITERATURE : One of the following periods :

   (i) *English literature up to 1550*
      History and criticism of English literature, including the early literature in translation, from the beginnings to 1550.

   (ii) *English literature and outstanding foreign literature available in English, 1550-1660*
      History and criticism of English literature from 1550-1660 ; outstanding foreign literature of the period, available in English by either contemporary or subsequent translation.

   (iii) *English literature and outstanding foreign literature available in English, 1660-1780*
      History and criticism of English literature from 1660-1780 ; outstanding foreign literature of the period, available in English by either contemporary or subsequent translation.

   (iv) *English and American literature and outstanding foreign literature available in English, 1780-1900*
      History and criticism of English and American literature from 1780-1900 ; outstanding foreign literature of the period, available in English by either contemporary or subsequent translation.

   (v) *English literature (including American literature and the literature of the British Commonwealth) and outstanding foreign literature available in English, 1900 onwards*
      History and criticism of English, American and British Commonwealth literature from 1900 onwards ; outstanding foreign literature of the period available in English.

3(b) PHILOSOPHY AND RELIGION

The publication of the results of modern scholarship. Periodicals : different types ; individual and collective indexes to them ; preprints and offprints, their purpose and their use and treatment in libraries ; abbreviations and forms of references ; catalogues of periodicals. Theses, " Programmschriften ", " Festschriften ". The publishing functions of learned societies and universities. Congresses. Co-operative works. Monographs and treatises. Series of texts and of monographs.

The leading reference books, handbooks and bibliographies. Current bibliographies and book reviews.

Philosophy. The works of outstanding European and American philosophers. Histories of philosophy. Manuals of philosophy and of particular branches of it. Reference books, bibliographies and book reviews. Periodicals.

Psychology. The chief schools of psychologists and the works of outstanding members of them. Reference books, bibliographies, abstracts and book reviews. Periodicals.

Christianity. The Bible : texts, versions, and commentaries. Patristics : series of editions and translations ; chief separate editions of the most important individual Fathers ; reference books. Classics of theology. Current theological writing. Church history : sources and handbooks. Devotional literature. Reference books ; bibliographies and book reviews. Periodicals.

The chief contemporary non-Christian religions. Judaism, Islam, Zoroastrianism, Hinduism, Buddhism, Confucianism, Taoism, Shinto : sacred books as far as available in English ; histories and treatises ; reference books. Primitive religion : outlines and standard treatises.

The comparative study of religion. Reference books and treatises.

Outstanding libraries and collections concerned with these subjects ; their contents, characteristics and facilities.

The treatment of these subjects in the principal general classification schemes (Dewey, U.D.C., Bliss, L.C.) and in special schemes for particular subjects.

Book-Selection. Policy as determined by clientele, by availability of other libraries, and by arrangements for inter-library loans. Sources and guides ; methods.

Reference work and assistance to readers.

3(c) SOCIAL SCIENCES (INCLUDING COMMERCE AND LAW)

The syllabus includes theoretical and applied economics (including commerce), sociology, political science, economic and commerical history, international affairs and law.

The standard treatises and periodicals, including the more important foreign material ; the publishing activities of the relevant institutions and societies ; government publications and their special problems of acquisition, cataloguing, arrangement, and use.

Economics. The principal writers on general theory, especially since the time of Adam Smith. The various " schools " of economists. The literature of particular topics (e.g. population, rent, tariffs) in their theoretical and practical aspects.

Statistics. As presented in the returns of governments and of international organizations, in dictionaries and periodicals and in the daily and weekly press.

Commerce and Industry. Commercial handbooks and directories, and other material for commercial intelligence. The literature of business organization. The organization and working of a commercial reference library, and of the library of a firm.

Sociology. The development of sociology (including social philosophy and social anthropology) as shown in the works of the principal writers. Social surveys, and other sources of information on social conditions.

Political science. Political philosophy and history of political ideas. The functions and technique of government, central and local, as set out in the main treatises and official documents.

Economic and commercial history. The main sources, primary and secondary, of English economic and commercial history from 1485 to the present day, with more detailed study of the period since 1800. The general trends of the economic development of the other great powers since 1815 as shown in the principal text-books.

International Affairs. Important documents concerning international events and problems, especially since 1914. The work of the great international organizations as shown in their publications.

Law. The elements of jurisprudence and English law, with special reference to the more important text-books and editions of the statutes and law reports. Bibliographical guides to legal publications. The bibliography of international law, particularly of treaties and the publications of the international courts. The main primary and secondary authorities on Roman law.

Outstanding libraries and collections in the social sciences; their contents, characteristics and facilities.

The treatment of these subjects in the principal general classification schemes (Dewey, U.D.C., L.C., Bliss); outstanding special classification schemes. Subject cataloguing of the literature of the social sciences.

Book-selection for different types of libraries in the field of the social sciences. Policy as determined by clientele, by availability of other libraries, and by inter-library loan schemes. Methods of book-selection. Methods of acquisition.

Reference work in the social sciences. Different types of enquirers and enquiries. The chief individual works of outstanding general importance in the categories mentioned above, their utility for different purposes, and the methods of using them. Presentation of results.

3(d) SCIENCE AND TECHNOLOGY

1st Paper : General Science

Science in ancient and medieval times, with special reference to the form of the works in which it was presented and to modern editions of them. Scientific treatises of the Renaissance, and the revival of ancient science. The rise of academies; their proceedings; other early periodicals; the literature of exploration; treatises and monographs of the seventeenth and eighteenth century. The multiplication of societies and periodicals; the great bibliographical collections; origin and growth of abstracting periodicals; publications of expeditions and surveys; development of treatises, etc. Histories of science; sources for biography of scientists.

Problems of scientific publication today. Publishing functions of scientific and professional societies. Scientific expeditions and surveys : form and content of their publications. Publications of research institutions. Theses.

Periodicals. The individual paper. Different types of periodicals. Individual and collective indexes. Preprints and offprints : their purposes and their use and treatment in libraries. Catalogues of periodicals. Abbreviations and forms of references.

Abstracts and abstract periodicals; coverage; language; indexes to abstracts. Book reviews. Current bibliographies. Reviews of progress : their different forms. Guides to the literature of particular subjects.

Monographs. Collections of tables and data. Treatises and " Handbücher " ; individual and collective authorship. Text-books. Popular scientific literature. Books on philosophy, functions, applications and organization of science.

Importance of different languages ; problems of translation ; technical dictionaries.

Scope and function of scientific societies, libraries and collections, professional institutions, and industrial research associations. The characteristics, facilities, and contents of important examples of each type.

The treatment of science in the principal general classification schemes (Dewey, U.D.C., L.C., Bliss) ; outstanding special classifications for science as a whole and for major branches of it. Subject cataloguing of scientific literature.

Book-selection for different types of scientific libraries. Policy as determined by clientele, by availability of other libraries and by inter-library loan schemes. Methods of book-selection. Methods of acquisition.

Methods of reference work in science. The chief individual works of outstanding general importance in the categories mentioned above, and their utility for different types of enquiry. Methods of making literature searches. Presentation of results.

2nd Paper : (i) *Mathematical and physical sciences, pure and applied (excluding chemistry)*

The syllabus covers mathematics, mechanics, astronomy, physics, electrical engineering.

Mathematics and mechanics. The principal mathematical treatises from classical times. Periodicals and societies. Abstracting periodicals and retrospective collections of abstracts. Bibliographies. Book-reviews, Guides to the literature.

Mathematical tables ; nomograms ; calculating machines. Societies and institutions ; libraries.

Astronomy. Treatises, periodicals. Abstracts, book reviews. Bibliographies. Collections of observations. Star-charts. Observatories, societies, institutions, libraries.

Physics. Outstanding early treatises. Periodicals. Abstracts, book reviews, bibliographies, reviews of progress. Current monographs, treatises, and " Handbücher ". Tables of constants. Societies and institutions. Libraries.

The syllabus covers the literature of special branches as well as that of physics in general.

Electrical Engineering, including telecommunications. Periodicals, scientific, trade, news, and house journals. Abstracts, book reviews, bibliographies. Monographs and treatises. Publications of firms. Patents, Societies, institutions, and firms. Libraries. Law relation to electrical engineering : principal textbooks, statutes, and statutory instruments.

or (ii) *Chemistry and chemical technology*

Pure chemistry. Outstanding early treatises. Periodicals. Abstracts, book reviews, bibliographies, reviews of progress. Guides to the literature.

Tables of constants.   Current monographs, treatises, and " Handbücher ". Societies and institutions.   Libraries.

Chemical technology.   Periodicals ;   trade, news, and house journals. Abstracts, book reviews, bibliographies, reviews of progress.   Guides to the literature.   Current monographs and treatises, and " Handbücher ". Publications of firms.   Patents.   Societies, institutions, and firms.   Libraries.   Factory law.   Principal text-books, statutes and statutory instruments.

The syllabus includes pure chemistry, chemical engineering, and the chief chemical industries—acid, alkali, coal, oil, plastics, food and drugs, and the metallurgical industries.

or (iii) *Natural history and biological sciences, pure and applied* (*excluding medicine*)

The syllabus covers geology and mineralogy, meteorology and climatology, biology (including genetics and cytology), botany and zoology (including bacteriology, mycology and parasitology), agriculture, horticulture, and forestry and silviculture.

Scientific expeditions.   Content and form of publication of their results ; general principles and individual examples of outstanding importance.

Geology and mineralogy (*including palaeontology*).   Outstanding early treatises.   Periodicals.   Geological surveys.   Form and content of their publications ;   general principles and individual examples of outstanding importance.   Geological maps.   Current monographs, treatises and " Handbücher ".   Abstracts, book reviews, bibliographies, reviews of progress.   Societies and institutions ;   mineralogical and palaeontological collections and their catalogues.   Libraries.

Meteorology and climatology.   Outstanding early treatises.   Periodicals. Collections of observations.   Current monographs, treatises, and " Handbücher ".   Abstracts, book reviews, bibliographies.   Societies, institutions, meteorological stations.   Libraries.

Biology (*including genetics, cytology, ecology, botany, zoology, bacteriology, mycology, parasitology*).   Outstanding early treatises.   Periodicals.   The literature of taxonomy ;   rules of nomenclature, publication of species, type specimens, indexes of genera and species, and of illustrations, local and general floras and faunas ;   monographs of particular groups.   Current monographs, treatises, " Handbücher ".   Abstracts, book reviews, bibliographies.   Reviews of progress.   Botanical and zoological gardens and museums ;   their publications.   Societies and institutions.   Libraries.

Agriculture, soil science, horticulture, forestry, silviculture (*excluding agricultural economics*).   Outstanding early treatises.   Periodicals, scientific, practical, and trade.   Current monographs, treatises, and reference books. Central and local government departments and their publications.   Research stations, and their publications.   Societies and their publications ;   herd books, etc.

or (iv) *Engineering* (*excluding electrical and chemical engineering*) *and building technology*

This syllabus covers mechanical, mining, civil and structural engineering, building technology, town and country planning.

Periodicals, professional, technical, and trade. Abstracts, book reviews. Standard specifications and codes of practice. Monographs and treatises. Collections of tables and data. Patents. Trade literature, catalogues, etc. Societies, institutions, and trade associations. Libraries. Law. Principal acts and statutory instruments. Control by local authorities ; bye-laws. Legal text-books, etc. Maps, plans, etc.

3(e) Fine Arts (excluding Music)

Aesthetics ; general criticism. General history of the arts. Primitive art. Religious art, Christian and non-Christian. Children's art. Industrial design.

Periodicals, English and foreign. Series and society publications. Indexes. Sale catalogues. Catalogues of galleries, museums and exhibitions. Catalogues raisonnés. Definitive editions. Bibliographies. Reference books. Biographical dictionaries.

Individual reproductions.

Graphic arts. History and development. Schools, groups, movements. Histories, general, national, and of particular periods. Forms and media, e.g. painting, engraving, drawing, caricature. Subjects, e.g. portraiture, landscape.

Sculpture. Topics as under Graphic arts, where applicable.

Architecture. Topics as under Graphic arts, where applicable.

Minor arts, such as pottery, glass, metalwork, furniture, jewellery, woodwork, tapestry, theatre décor.

Galleries, museums, and exhibitions. Private collectors and collections. Societies and councils. Education, schools, study and teaching. Art libraries ; collections of reproductions.

Book selection. Policy. Sources and guides. Methods. Evaluation of books for different purposes, e.g. as popular, factual, critical.

Classification ; cataloguing. The application of the principal general schemes (Dewey, U.D.C., Bliss, L.C.) to the literature of art ; special schemes ; comparisons. Problems of cross-division in classifying art books. Arrangement on shelves. Types of catalogues. Analytics. Special problems of subject cataloguing.

Care and custody. Storage and shelving. Binding. Collating. Single prints, drawings, and reproductions ; mounting ; portfolios. Ownership marks. Prevention of loss and mutilation. Exhibition.

3(f) Music

General musical history ; the history of special periods, countries or schools of composition ; the work of particular composers or musical scholars ; musical psychology and aesthetics ; the meaning of musical terms ; the history of musical form ; the development of musical instruments ; the history of musical notation ; music printing and publishing ; the technique of musical editing ; musical copyright ; recorded music ; the great libraries and collections of music, their history, character and facilities ; the selection of music for library stocks ; the cataloguing, classification and shelving of music ; musical reference books, includin bibliographies, dictionaries, thematic and other catalogues, the standard histories and biographies and the chief collected editions of the works of the great composers.

Candidates will be expected to show that they have sufficient first-hand acquaintance with what has been written in the various forms to be able to make a good choice of music for performance or study and to express opinions of their own on musical styles and tendencies.

3(g) MEDICINE

Medical Library Practice. History and development of medical libraries throughout the world. Lives and achievements of famous medical bibliographers and librarians. Present state of medical libraries in Great Britain : libraries of corporations, societies, universities and colleges, hospitals and medical schools, government departments, firms, and research institutions. Special collections. Organization, administration and functions of medical libraries. Staff selection and training. Selection of books and periodicals. Service to different categories of readers (research workers, students, etc.). Provision for non-medical readers. Relations with the general public. Bibliographical services. Reference and enquiry work. Abstracting and translating services. Reprints, pamphlets, theses. Bibliographical citation and proof correcting ; abbreviations. Indexing of medical books and periodicals. The treatment of medicine in the principal general classification schemes (Dewey, U.D.C., L.C., Bliss) ; outstanding special classifications for medicine as a whole and for major branches of it. Subject cataloguing of medical literature.

The Literature of Medicine. Outlines of medical history, with special reference to bibliographical landmarks. Histories and bibliographies of medicine (ancient and modern) and guides to the literature of particular subjects. Main outlines of the literature of dentistry, veterinary medicine, pharmacy, and nursing. Current bibliographies, annuals, year books, reviews of progress. Index-Catalogue of the Surgeon-General's Library, Index, Medicus, Quarterly Cumulative Index Medicus, Current List of Medical Literature. Other library catalogues and indexes. The various types of medical periodicals and the indexes to them. Abstracting journals. Encyclopaedias, loose-leaf systems of medicine, text-books, monographs, " Festschriften ", " Handbücher ", theses, pharmacopoeias, etc. Congresses and conferences. Medical nomenclature. Dictionaries of medical terms in English and other languages. The original descriptions of diseases and their treatment. Eponyms. Commemorative orations and lectures. Sources of medical biography. Individual bibliographies of medical writers. Government publications. Vital statistics. Reports of medical officers of health. Publications of the League of Nations and of the World Health Organization.

3(h) HISTORY AND ARCHAEOLOGY

The syllabus covers ancient, medieval and modern European history and archaeology.

The publication of the results of modern scholarship. Periodicals : different types ; individual and collective indexes to them ; preprints and offprints, their purpose and their use and treatment in libraries ; abbreviations and forms of references ; catalogues of periodicals. Theses, " Programmschriften ", " Festschriften ". The publishing functions of learned societies and universities. Congresses. Co-operative works. Monographs and treatises. Series of texts and of monographs.

The leading reference books, handbooks and bibliographies. Books on the history and method of scholarship. Current bibliographies, book reviews, and reviews of progress.

Historical sources. Archive and similar material ; published guides to it and modern editions of it ; problems of cataloguing and arrangement. Use (but not custody and care) of manuscript material. Chronicles. Memoirs.

The development of historiography. Outstanding recent histories and historical biographies.

Biographical, topographical, and iconographic reference books and sources.

Methods of chronology ; chronological tables.

Historical atlases.

Archaeology. Expeditions and excavations, their methods and the publication of their results. "Corpora" of inscriptions, coins, vases, etc. Archaeological museums, their catalogues and other publications.

Outstanding libraries and collections concerned with these subjects ; their contents, characteristics and facilities.

The treatment of these subjects in the principal general classification schemes (Dewey, U.D.C., Bliss, L.C.) and in special schemes for particular subjects.

Book-selection. Policy as determined by clientele, by availability of other libraries, and by arrangements for inter-library loans. Sources and guides ; methods.

Reference work and assistance to readers.

3(i) General and European Philology

The syllabus requires a general knowledge of linguistics (general and European), the history of European literature, and literary theory and scholarship, and more particularly of their bibliographical aspects and the peculiar problems of libraries concerned with them.

Linguistics. The broad outlines of the development and divisions of linguistic science, of the linguistic history of Europe, and of the relationships and chief characteristics of the several European languages, including a knowledge of the work of the most important scholars. (No questions will be set which require a detailed knowledge of the philology of any specified language, or of the literature relating thereto.)

Special products of linguistic scholarship (grammars, dictionaries, atlases, sound recordings) : their development, characteristics and uses.

Literature. The main movements and genres in European literature, classical, medieval and modern, considered from the point of view of bibliography and scholarship.

The outlines of the development of literary aesthetics and criticism : theories and schools ; the significance and chief publications of the major critics.

The task and methods of literary scholarship—textual criticism as related to book-production, ancient and modern, interpretation ; literary biography and history ; background studies. Candidates will be expected to be acquainted with the work of outstanding scholars in the fields of Latin, Greek, French, Italian, Spanish and German literature, but otherwise no questions will be set which require a detailed knowledge of the scholarship relating to particular literatures.

The sources, manuscript and otherwise, of literary texts. Collections and catalogues.

Bibliographical aspects. The forms of scholarly production—periodicals, theses, Programmschriften, Festchriften, proceedings of congresses, series of texts and monographs : their characteristics, treatment and uses.

The leading bibliographies, reference books, handbooks, periodicals and reviews of progress in the field of general linguistics, literature, and Classical, Romance and Germanic philology.

Outstanding libraries and collections : their contents, characteristics and facilities.

Librarianship. The application of the above to the questions of book-selection (including policy as determined by clientele, co-operation and availability of other libraries), cataloguing, classification (including the treatment of the subjects in Dewey, U.D.C., Bliss, L.C. and Colon), and reference work.

FINAL, PART 4.   One of the following :   *(Two papers of 3 hours)*

4(a) Palaeography and Archives

Archives and Administration : Definition ; provenance ; classification and location of English archive accumulations. Care and custody of archives ; methods of storage and repair ; arrangement, listing and making available to the public. Private muniments. Bibliography.

Forms and Handwritings of English Documents : from the Conquest to the present day. Handwritings of Western Europe ; development of hand-writing and documentary form in England in royal and ecclesiastical administrations. Court hand ; official scribes, notaries, scriveners and writing masters. The private Deed. Bibliography.

Tests in Transcribing and Annotating Latin, Anglo-Norman and English documents ; and in *translation* from Latin and Anglo-Norman.

(Intending candidates for this Part may borrow photostats of documents used in previous examinations on application to the Secretary.)

4(b) Library Work with Young People

1st Paper

Literature. History and criticism of English literature for children : outstanding foreign literature, together with a detailed knowledge of the best modern books in all branches of children's literature. Carnegie medal and other awards. Reference material. Books suitable to various ages and for backward children. Bibliographies and other aids to book selection. Surveys of reading. History and present trends in book production. Aids to reading, including visual aids. Methods of cataloguing and arranging books in libraries.

Child and Adolescent Psychology. Child behaviour. Mental growth. Linguistic and reading ability of the child at various ages. Social development. Backward children. Adolescent psychology.

2nd Paper

Planning, Equipment, Organization and Development. History and development in the British Isles. General development abroad, including knowledge of children's work in U.S.A. Planning and equipment. Administration and methods. Circulation and reference methods. Extension activities. Liaison work with schools and outside organizations. Children's library work in rural areas.

Education and Educational Institutions. Outline of the history of education in the United Kingdom, including general provisions of the 1944 Act. Aims and book needs of various types of schools and colleges, including primary and secondary schools, county colleges, youth clubs, etc. Responsibilities of Local Education Authorities. School libraries and school librarians. Planning, administration and methods. Book selection related to the curriculum, recreation reading and special interests. Subsidiary material such as illustrations and periodicals. Co-operation with outside organizations.

4(c) Advanced Classification and Cataloguing

1st Paper : Classification

The theory of classification. History of bibliographical classification with special reference to the period 1876 to date : main schemes, their development and principles. Practice of classification in general and research libraries. Methods of compiling schemes for particular purposes. The limits and problems of classification. The planning and working of a classification department and its relations with cataloguing. Codes. Application to material other than books. Guiding and display. Punched cards and other mechanical aids in connection with classification and cataloguing.

2nd Paper : Cataloguing

The history of cataloguing and the comparative study of the chief codes of rules. The principles of cataloguing and their application to general and special problems. Advanced cataloguing practice with particular reference to the dictionary, classified and name catalogues. Subject headings. Construction of indexes. Annotation. Physical forms of catalogues. The planning and working of a cataloguing department.

4(d) Historical Bibliography

History of printing and the evolution of the book. The history and use of papyrus, vellum, parchment and paper. History of binding and binding decoration. Book illustration from the decoration of the MS. to modern methods. History of authorship, publishing and bookselling. The censorship of the Press. The Stationers' Company. Copyright. The growth of trade bibliography.

4(e) PRESENTATION AND DISSEMINATION OF INFORMATION

Presentation of ideas, including composition, style and language, readership, choice of material. Types of publications : reviews, house journals, annual reports, etc., and methods of reproduction and printing of them. Editing, including law of libel. Preparation for the press. Copyright in dissemination. Abstracting and the form of abstract journals, preparation of reports and publicity material. Collation of abstracts with originals. The principles and practice of indexing in special libraries, and the recent developments in mechanical and electronic methods.

4(f) LITERATURE OF WALES

The scope of this examination is intended to be wide enough to comprehend all the Welsh subjects essential to a librarian having to administer a Welsh collection. It therefore includes not only Welsh literature but also books about Wales, Welsh history, and kindred subjects as reflected in printed books. Acquaintance with essential bibliographical " tools " is expected. At least two questions must be answered in Welsh.

1st Paper : Welsh Literature

A general knowledge of Welsh literature of all periods with particular attention to the four centuries of Welsh printed books, including nineteenth- and twentieth-century periodical literature and the journals of learned societies and religious bodies. Twentieth-century " Anglo-Welsh " literature.

2nd Paper : Welsh history and antiquities, topography and travel

A general knowledge of printed works bearing on the above topics, including church, political, social, economic, and local history. " Tours in Wales ", particularly from 1770 to 1830.

POST-GRADUATE SYLLABUS: A special note

At the meeting of the Council held on October 30th, 1964, it was decided to introduce a post-graduate syllabus to operate from 1966 onwards. Details of this syllabus appeared in the L.A. Record for January 1965 : but at the time of going to press the regulations and other administrative details were not available. They will be published in the L.A. Record from time to time, and incorporated in the Students' handbook for 1966-67.

SPECIMEN CATALOGUE ENTRIES

Below are some forms of setting out entries which are acceptable to the examiners for questions 1 and 2 in Part II, B 13. The use of main entries as unit entries is permissible.

Candidates are advised to adopt one of these styles and to use it consistently throughout their practical work.

Classified Catalogue

MAIN ENTRY

[Class no.]

Frayne, John G   , *and* Wolfe, Halley.
    Elements of sound recording [by] John G. Frayne, . . . [and] Halley Wolfe. . . . New York, John Wiley & sons inc.; London, Chapman & Hall, ltd., 1949.
        vii, [1], 686 p. illus., tables, diagrs.   23½cm.
        Bibliographies, graphs.
        [Annotation]

AUTHOR INDEX

Frayne, John G   , *and* Wolfe, Halley.
    Elements of sound recording.   1949.

[Class no.]

Wolfe, Halley, *joint author.*
    Elements of sound recording [by] John G. Frayne, . . . [and] Halley Wolfe.   1949.

[Class no.]

        or

Wolfe, Halley, *joint author.*
    Frayne, John G   , *and* Wolfe, Halley.
        Elements of sound recording.   1949.

[Class no.]

        or

Wolfe, Halley, *joint author.*
    see

Frayne, John G   , *and* Wolfe, Halley.
    Elements of sound recording . . .

SUBJECT INDEX

Sound recording

[Class no.]

Recording, Sound

[Class no.]

Dictionary Catalogue

MAIN ENTRY

Martin, L   H   , *and* Hill, R   D   .
    A manual of vacuum practice by L. H. Martin, . . . and R. D. Hill. . . .
Melbourne, University press, 1948. [1947.]
      x, 120 p. 3 pl., tables, 56 diagrs. 19 cm.
      Bibliographies.

                                                 [Class no.]

    [Annotation]

ADDED ENTRY OR REFERENCE

Hill, R   D   , *joint author*.
    A manual of vacuum practice by L. H. Martin, . . . and R. D. Hill. 1948
                                               [Class no.]

      or

Hill, R   D   , *joint author*.
    Martin, L   H   , *and* Hill, R   D   .
      A manual of vacuum practice. 1948.

                                               [Class no.]

      or

Hill, R   D   , *joint author*.
    see
    Martin, L   H   , *and* Hill, R   D   .
      A manual of vacuum practice . . .

SUBJECT ENTRY

    Vacuums
      Martin, L   H   , *and* Hill, R   D   .
        A manual of vacuum practice. 1948.

                                               [Class no.]

EXAMINATION CENTRES AND METHOD OF ENTRY PROCEDURE

Full particulars regarding entry procedure, together with the current list of examination centres, are published in the LIBRARY ASSOCIATION RECORD *in February and August, for the Summer and Winter Examinations respectively.*

CONDUCT OF EXAMINATIONS

The examinations are supervised for the Council by the Board of Assessors, which is responsible for the approval of question papers, the final assessment of scripts and the publication of results. The setting of questions and the marking of candidates' answers are the responsibility of a Senior Examiner, helped by Assistant Examiners when necessary, and supervised by a Subject Assessor. Borderline scripts are carefully checked at each stage before final marking is confirmed.

The prescribed marking is as follows :

Part I Examination. Each Paper will be marked from a maximum of 100 marks. To Pass, a candidate must either (*a*) obtain 50 marks in each of the four Papers *or* (*b*) Pass in three Papers with an aggregate of 220 marks in the four Papers. A candidate must pass the Examination at a single sitting, but he may be Referred to his studies in one Paper if he has passed in three Papers and obtained an aggregate of 200 marks in the whole examination. A candidate who subsequently Fails in a Paper in which he has been Referred will be required to take the whole of the Part I Examination again.

Part II Examination. Each Paper will be marked from 100 marks, except in the case of B 21, which is a 6-hour paper in two sections, which will be marked as a whole from an aggregate of 200 marks, and a pass in which will count as passes in two Papers.

In both Part I and Part II, 50% will give a Pass, 70% a Merit, and 85% Honours.

Entrance Examination. Each Paper will be marked from a total of 60 marks. A candidate will pass the Examination if he obtains an aggregate of 120 marks. Honours or Merit is given for a Pass in four Papers with a total of 200 or 160 marks respectively.

LIST OF ASSESSORS AND EXAMINERS

(As at November 16th, 1964.)

BOARD OF ASSESSORS
Miss L. V. Paulin, M.A., F.L.A.
Mr. T. E. Callander, F.L.A.
Professor R. Irwin, M.A., F.L.A.
Mr. K. A. Mallaber, F.L.A.
Mr. W. Tynemouth, F.L.A. *(Chairman)*.

PART I, PAPERS 1, 2, 3 and 4
    Assessor :   Mr. E. A. Clough, F.L.A.

PART I, PAPER 1 (The Library and the community)
Senior Examiner :	Mr. R. Staveley, B.A., F.L.A.
Assistant Senior Examiner :	Mr. K. C. Harrison, M.B.E., F.L.A.
Assistant Examiners :	Mr. B. M. Charlton, F.L.A.
	Mr. W. R. Flint, F.L.A.
	Mr. R. H. Hassell, F.L.A.
	Mr. C. Jones, B.A., F.L.A.
	Mr. A. O. Meakin, F.L.A.
	Mr. A. D. Mortimore, M.A., F.L.A.
	Mr. P. D. Pocklington, F.L.A.
	Mr. R. Sturt, F.L.A.
	Mr. G. Thomas, B.A., F.L.A.
	Mr. L. White, F.L.A.

PART I, PAPER 2 (Government and control of libraries)
Senior Examiner :	Mr. E. V. Corbett, F.L.A.
Assistant Senior Examiner :	Mr. D. T. Richnell, B.A., F.L.A.
Assistant Examiners :	Mr. W. H. Aitken, F.L.A.
	Mr. D. J. Bryant, F.L.A.
	Mr. F. Cochrane, F.L.A., D.G.A.
	Mr. G. Jefferson, F.L.A.
	Mr. K. Lund, F.L.A.
	Mr. F. Taylor, F.L.A.
	Mr. W. T. Woods, F.L.A.

PART I, PAPER 3 (The Organization of knowledge)
Senior Examiner :	Mr. L. G. Lovell, F.L.A.
Assistant Senior Examiner :	Mr. J. W. Cockburn, F.L.A.
Assistant Examiners :	Mr. S. F. Harper, F.L.A.
	Mr. F. M. Jorysz, B.A., F.L.A.
	Mrs. E. Knowles, F.L.A.
	Mr. A. Maltby, F.L.A.
	Mr. J. C. Powell, F.L.A.
	Mr. J. F. W. Sherwood, F.L.A., A.M.A.
	Mr. J. A. Tait, M.A., F.L.A.

PART I, PAPER 4 (Bibliographical control and service)
Senior Examiner :	Mr. J. T. Gillett, F.L.A.
Assistant Senior Examiner :	Mr. W. B. Stevenson, F.L.A.
Assistant Examiners :	Mrs. A. Bakewell, F.L.A.
	Mr. J. A. Dearden, F.L.A.
	Mr. R. E. Grimshaw, F.L.A.
	Mr. S. H. Horrocks, F.L.A.
	Mr. I. M. Jamieson, F.L.A.
	Mr. G. Mort, F.L.A.
	Mr. V. G. Turner, F.L.A.
	Mr. K. Whittaker, F.L.A.

PART II. *Assessor :*   Mr. K. A. Mallaber, F.L.A.

PART II, LIST A, PAPERS 1, 2 and 3
Subject Assessor :   Mr. W. Tynemouth, F.L.A.

PART II, LIST A, PAPER 1 (Academic and copyright libraries)
Senior Examiner :	Mr. D. T. Richnell, B.A., F.L.A.
Assistant Senior Examiner :	Mr. F. J. Hill, M.A., F.L.A.
Assistant Examiners :	

PART II, LIST A, PAPER 2 (Special libraries and information bureaux)
Senior Examiner :	Mr. L. G. Patrick, F.L.A.
Assistant Senior Examiner :	Mr. H. H. Goom, A.L.A.
Assistant Examiners :	

PART II, LIST A, PAPER 3 (Public (municipal and county) libraries)
Senior Examiner :	Mr. E. A. Clough, F.L.A.
Assistant Senior Examiner :	Mr. D. G. Williams, F.L.A.
Assistant Examiners :	Mr. E. T. Bryant, F.L.A.
	Mr. H. C. Cullum, F.L.A.
	Mr. J. Hoyle, F.L.A.
	Mr. T. Mann, F.L.A.
	Mr. J. Neill, F.L.A.
	Mr. F. C. Pritchard, F.L.A.
	Mr. O. S. Tomlinson, F.L.A.
	Mr. L. G. Tootell, F.L.A.

PART II, LIST B, PAPER 11 (Theory of classification)
Subject Assessor :	Mr. S. J. Butcher, F.L.A.
Senior Examiner :	Mr. E. R. J. Hawkins, F.L.A.
Assistant Senior Examiner :	Mr. C. A. Part, F.L.A.
Assistant Examiners :	Mr. K. G. B. Bakewell, F.L.A.
	Mr. B. Hunnisett, F.L.A.
	Mr. N. Taylor, F.L.A.
	Mr. A. M. Windsor, F.L.A.

PART II, LIST B, PAPER 12 (Theory of cataloguing)
    Subject Assessor :   Mr. S. J. Butcher, F.L.A.
    Senior Examiner :   Mr. E. F. Ferry, F.L.A.
    Assistant Senior Examiner :   Mr. H. E. Radford, F.L.A.
    Assistant Examiners :   Mr. A. C. Butler, B.A., F.L.A.
                               Mr. W. Critchley, F.L.A.
                               Mr. F. McAdams, F.L.A.
                               Mr. R. C. Rider, B.A., F.L.A.

PART II, LIST B, PAPER 13 (Practical classification and cataloguing)
    Subject Assessor :   Mr. S. J. Butcher, F.L.A.
    Senior Examiner :   Mr. R. F. Vollans, F.L.A.
    Assistant Senior Examiner :   Mr. W. R. Maidment, F.L.A.
    Assistant Examiners :   Mr. A. B. Craven, F.L.A.
                               Mr. K. G. E. Harris, M.A., F.L.A.
                               Mr. L. J. Shaw, F.L.A.
                               Mr. A. Wilson, F.L.A.

PART II, LIST B, PAPER 21 (Bibliography)
    Subject Assessor :   Mr. T. E. Callander, F.L.A.
    Senior Examiner :   Mr. P. R. Lewis, F.L.A.
    Assistant Senior Examiner :   Mr. R. J. Roberts, M.A., A.L.A.
    Assistant Examiners :   Miss L. V. Baird, B.A., F.L.A.
                               Mr. R. Blundell, F.L.A.
                               Mr. L. Bulmer, B.A., Dip. Ed., F.L.A.
                               Mr. K. L. Gibson, B.A., F.L.A.
                               Mr. P. Hepworth, M.A., F.L.A.
                               Mr. G. E. Laughton, F.L.A.
                               Mr. F. N. McDonald, F.L.A.
                               Mr. E. W. Padwick, F.L.A.
                               Mr. A. J. Simpson, F.L.A.
                               Mr. S. H. Tennent, F.L.A.
                               Mr. G. O. Turner, F.L.A.
                               Mr. P. K. J. Wright, F.L.A.
                               Mr. E. R. Yescombe, F.L.A.

PART II, LIST B, PAPER 22 (History of libraries and librarianship)
    Subject Assessor :   Professor R. Irwin, M.A., F.L.A.
    Senior Examiner :   Miss C. R. Lutyens, F.L.A.
    Assistant Senior Examiner :   Mr. K. W. Humphreys, B.Litt., M.A.
    Assistant Examiners :

PART II, LIST B, PAPER 31 (Handling and dissemination of information)
    Subject Assessor :   Mr. D. V. Arnold, B.Sc., F.L.A.
    Senior Examiner :   Mr. W. Ashworth, B.Sc., A.R.P.S., F.L.A.
    Assistant Senior Examiner :   Mr. J. R. Sharp, F.L.A.
    Assistant Examiner :   Mr. R. G. Surridge, F.L.A. (reserve)

PART II, LIST B, PAPER 32 (Library service for young people in schools and public libraries)

Subject Assessor :	Miss D. D. Chilcot, F.L.A.
Senior Examiner :	Miss B. M. L. Brazier, F.L.A.
Assistant Senior Examiner :	Miss E. N. Bewick, A.L.A.
Assistant Examiners :	Mr. A. M. Morley, A.L.A.
	Mrs. F. Sturt, F.L.A.

PART II, List B, PAPER 33 (Hospital libraries)

Subject Assessor :	Mr. W. Tynemouth, F.L.A.
Senior Examiner :	Mr. R. Sturt, F.L.A.
Assistant Senior Examiner :	
Assistant Examiners :	

PART II, LIST B, PAPER 91 (Archive administration and records management)

Subject Assessor :	Professor R. Irwin, M.A., F.L.A.
Senior Examiner :	Mr. G. F. Osborn, F.L.A.
Assistant Senior Examiner :	Miss J. M. Gibbs, B.A.
Assistant Examiners :	

PART II, LIST B, PAPER 92 (Palaeography and diplomatic)

Subject Assessor :	Professor R. Irwin, M.A., F.L.A.
Senior Examiner :	Mr. G. F. Osborn, F.L.A.
Assistant Senior Examiner :	Miss J. M. Gibbs, B.A.

PART II, LIST C, PAPER 101 (. . . Old and Middle English, to 1400)

Subject Assessor :	Miss C. H. W. Bickle, B.A., F.L.A.
Senior Examiner :	Mr. K. W. Humphreys, B.Litt., M.A.
Assistant Senior Examiner :	

PART II, LIST C, PAPER 102 (. . . English literature, 1400-1800)

Subject Assessor :	Miss C. H. W. Bickle, B.A., F.L.A.
Senior Examiner :	Mr. R. A. Bangs, B.A., F.L.A.
Assistant Senior Examiner :	Mr. A. H. Smith, B.A., F.L.A.
Assistant Examiners :	Mrs. M. Bithell, M.A., F.L.A.
	Mr. N. Carrick, B.A., F.L.A.
	Mr. J. C. Haywood, F.L.A.
	Mr. M. H. Statham, M.A., F.L.A.

PART II, LIST C, PAPER 103 (. . . Literature in English, 1750-date)

Subject Assessor :	Miss C. H. W. Bickle, B.A., F.L.A.
Senior Examiner :	Mr. J. Thompson, B.A., A.L.A.
Assistant Senior Examiner :	Mr. B. J. Moore, B.A., F.L.A.
Assistant Examiner :	Mr. B. L. Pearce, F.L.A.

PART II, LIST C, PAPER 106 (. . . Literature for children)
Subject Assessor :   Miss D. D. Chilcot, F.L.A.
Senior Examiner :   Miss B. M. L. Brazier, F.L.A.
Assistant Senior Examiner :   Miss E. N. Bewick, A.L.A.
Assistant Examiner :   Miss A. M. Parker, A.L.A.

PART II, LIST C, PAPER 108 (. . . Welsh language and literature)
Subject Assessor :   Mr. E. D. Jones, B.A., F.S.A.
Senior Examiner :   Mr. A. R. Edwards, F.L.A.

For the following specialist Papers Subject Assessors will be appointed as and when necessary :

PART II, LIST C, PAPER 109 (. . . French language and literature)
Subject Assessor :
Senior Examiner :   Mr. P. Havard-Williams, M.A., A.L.A., A.N.Z.L.A.

PART II, LIST C, PAPER 110 (. . . Spanish language and literature)
Subject Assessor :
Senior Examiner :   Mr. B. J. Moore, B.A., F.L.A.

PART II, LIST C, PAPER 111 (. . . Italian language and literature)
Subject Assessor :
Senior Examiner :   Mr. F. S. Stych, M.A., F.L.A.

PART II, LIST C, PAPER 112 (. . . German language and literature)
Subject Assessor :
Senior Examiner :   Mr. A. J. Dickson, B.A., A.K.C., F.L.A.

PART II, LIST C, PAPER 113 (. . . General and Indo-European philology)
Subject Assessor :
Senior Examiner :   Dr. A. J. Walford, M.A., F.L.A.

PART II, LIST C, PAPER 114 (. . . Classics . . .)
Subject Assessor :
Senior Examiner :

PART II, LIST C, PAPER 115 (. . . Russian language and literature)
Subject Assessor :
Senior Examiner :   Mr. J. S. G. Simmons, M.B.E., M.A.

PART II, LIST C, PAPER 201 (. . . Archaeology and ancient history)
Subject Assessor :
Senior Examiner :   Mr. R. W. P. Wyatt, B.A., F.L.A.
Assistant Examiner :   Mr. P. A. Clayton, F.R.N.S., F.L.A., Dip.Arch. (reserve)

PART II, LIST C, PAPER 202 (. . . Medieval and modern history)
Subject Assessor :
Senior Examiner :   Mr. C. Muris, M.A., F.L.A.
Assistant Senior Examiner :   Mr. P. S. Morrish, B.A., A.K.C., A.L.A.

PART II, LIST C, PAPER 203 (. . . Geography)
Subject Assessor :
Senior Examiner :
Senior Examiner :   Mr. G. Walters, B.Sc., F.L.A.

PART II, LIST C, PAPER 301 (Religion)
Subject Assessor :
Senior Examiner :   Miss M. Johnson, M.A., F.L.A.

PART II, LIST C, PAPER 302 (. . . Philosophy . . .)
Subject Assessor :
Senior Examiner :   Rev. R. P. D. Thomas, M.A.

PART II, LIST C, PAPER 303 (. . . Education)
Subject Assessor :   Mr. D. J. Foskett, M.A., F.L.A.
Senior Examiner :   Mr. J. D. Dews, M.A., F.L.A.

Assistant Senior Examiner :

PART II, LIST C, PAPER 304 (. . . Sociology)
Subject Assessor :   Mr. K. A. Mallaber, F.L.A.
Senior Examiner :   Mr. W. L. Saunders, M.A., F.L.A.

PART II, LIST C, PAPER 305 (Political Science and Law)
Subject Assessor :   Mr. K. A. Mallaber, F.L.A.
Senior Examiner :   Mr. K. G. Harris, M.A., F.L.A.

PART II, LIST C, PAPER 306 (. . . Economics)
Subject Assessor :   Mr. K. A. Mallaber, F.L.A.
Senior Examiner :   Mr. P. R. Lewis, F.L.A.

PART II, LIST C, PAPER 401 (. . . Fine Arts . . .)
Subject Assessor :
Senior Examiner :   Mr. N. Carrick, B.A., F.L.A.

PART II, LIST C, PAPER 402 (. . . Music)
Subject Assessor :   Dr. C. B. Oldman, C.V.O., C.B., M.A., F.S.A., F.L.A.
Senior Examiner :   Mr. R. L. W. Collison, F.L.A.
Assistant Senior Examiner :   Miss J. Houlgate, A.L.A., L.R.A.M.
Assistant Examiner :   Miss A. E. Rowley, B.A., F.L.A. (reserve)

PART II, LIST C, PAPER 501 (. . . Mechanical engineering)
    Subject Assessor :   Mr. W. Ashworth, B.Sc., A.R.P.S., F.L.A.
    Senior Examiner :   Mr. J. Stephenson, F.L.A.
    Assistant Senior Examiner :   Mr. C. A. Wise, F.L.A.

PART II, LIST C, PAPER 502 (. . . Civil engineering, building and mining engineering)
    Subject Assessor :   Mr. W. Ashworth, B.Sc., A.R.P.S., F.L.A.
    Senior Examiner :   Mr. K. G. Turner, A.L.A.

PART II, LIST C, PAPER 503 (. . . Electrical engineering)
    Subject Assessor :   Mr. W. Ashworth, B.Sc., A.R.P.S., F.L.A.
    Senior Examiner :   Miss E. Vallender, F.L.A.

PART II, LIST C, PAPER 504 (History of Science, and technology, 1600 to date)
    Subject Assessor :   Mr. W. Ashworth, B.Sc., A.R.P.S., F.L.A.
    Senior Examiner :   Mr. K. D. C. Vernon, F.L.A.
    Assistant Senior Examiner :

PART II, LIST C, PAPER 505 (. . . Chemistry and chemical technology)
    Subject Assessor :   Mr. W. Ashworth, B.Sc., A.R.P.S., F.L.A.
    Senior Examiner :   Mr. R. G. Griffin, F.L.A.

PART II, LIST C, PAPER 506 (. . . Natural history and biological sciences)
    Subject Assessor :   Mr. W. Ashworth, B.Sc., A.R.P.S., F.L.A.
    Senior Examiner :   Mr. A. C. Townsend, M.A.

PART II, LIST C, PAPER 507 (. . . Medicine)
    Subject Assessor :
    Senior Examiner :   Mr. L. T. Morton, F.L.A.

PART II, LIST C, PAPER 601 (. . . Africa . . .)
    Subject Assessor :
    Senior Examiner :   Mr. E. E. Burke, F.L.A.

PART II, LIST C, PAPER 602 (. . . Near East . . .)
Subject Assessor :
Senior Examiner :   Mr. M. F. Holloway, M.A., F.L.A.

PART II, LIST C, PAPER 603 (. . . South Asia . . .)
Subject Assessor :
Senior Examiner :   Mr. M. R. Jain, M.A., F.L.A.

PART II, LIST C, PAPER 604 (. . . Far East . . .)
Subject Assessor :
Senior Examiner :   Mr. A. F. Johnson, F.L.A., L.R.S.M.

PART II, LIST C, PAPER 605 (. . . Caribbean Region)
Subject Assessor :
Senior Examiner :   Mr. K. E. Ingram, B.A., F.L.A.

ENTRANCE EXAMINATION
    Subject Assessor :   Mr. T. E. Callander, F.L.A.
    Senior Examiners :
        Papers 1 and 2   Mr. H. Sargeant, F.L.A.
        Papers 3 and 4   Mr. E. L. J. Smith, F.L.A.
    Senior Assistant Examiners :
        Papers 1 and 2   Mr. R. N. Lock, F.L.A.
        Papers 3 and 4   Mr. S. J. Green, F.L.A.
    Assistant Examiners :
        Papers 1 and 2   Mr. H. K. G. Bearman, F.L.A.
                                       Mr. R. Helliwell, F.L.A.
                                       Mr. J. S. Parsonage, F.L.A.
                                       Mr. W. D. Pigott, F.L.A.
                                       Mr. J. Sankey, F.L.A.
                                       Mr. K. Smith, F.L.A.
                                       Mr. K. A. Stockham, F.L.A.
                                       Mr. J. N. Taylor, F.L.A.
                                       Mr. H. Ward, F.L.A.
                                       Mr. L. White, F.L.A.
        Papers 3 and 4   Mr. R. B. Bateman, F.L.A.
                                       Mr. B. C. Bennett, F.L.A.
                                       Mr. W. Critchley, F.L.A.
                                       Mr. D. E. Davinson, F.L.A.
                                       Mr. J. Dove, F.L.A., F.R.C.O.,
                                           A.R.C.M.
                                       Mr. D. E. Gray, F.L.A.
                                       Mr. H. E. Taylor, F.L.A.
                                       Mr. S. J. Teague, F.L.A.

1950 FINAL PART 1 (Bibliography, etc.)
    Subject Assessor :   Mr. T. E. Callander, F.L.A.
    Senior Examiner :   Mr. R. E. Grimshaw, F.L.A.
    Senior Assistant Examiner : Mr. G. E. Hamilton, F.L.A.

1950 FINAL PART 2 (Organization and Administration)
    Subject Assessor :   Mr. W. Tynemouth, F.L.A.
    1st Paper (General)
    Senior Examiner :   Dr. W. A. Munford, M.B.E., B.Sc.
                                      (Econ.), F.L.A.

    2nd Paper (a)
    Senior Examiner :   Mr. E. A. Clough, F.L.A.
    Senior Assistant Examiner : Mr. D. G. Williams, F.L.A.
    2nd Paper (b)
    Senior Examiner :   Mr. D. T. Richnell, B.A., F.L.A.
    2nd Paper (c)
    Senior Examiner :   Mr. L. G. Patrick, F.L.A.

1950 FINAL PART 3 (Literature and librarianship of special subjects)
    (a) (English Literature)
    Subject Assessor :   Miss C. H. W. Bickle, B.A., F.L.A.
    Senior Examiners :   (i) Mr. K. W. Humphreys, B.Litt., M.A.
                        (ii) Mr. J. F. T. Thomson, M.A., F.L.A.
                      (iii) Mr. V. T. H. Parry, M.A., F.L.A.
                      (iv) Mr. J. F. T. Thomson, M.A., F.L.A.
                      (v) Mr. D. E. Gerard, B.A., F.L.A.
    (b) (Philosophy and Religion)
    Subject Assessor :   Professor R. Irwin, M.A., F.L.A.
    Senior Examiner :   Rev. R. P. D. Thomas, M.A.
    (c) (Social Sciences—including commerce and law)
    Subject Assessor :   Mr. K. A. Mallaber, F.L.A.
    Senior Examiner :   Mr. W. L. Saunders, M.A., F.L.A.
    (d) (Science and Technology)
    Subject Assessor :   Mr. W. Ashworth, B.Sc., A.R.P.S.,
                                      F.L.A.

    Senior Examiners :
        1st Paper   Mr. K. D. C. Vernon, F.L.A.
        2nd Paper   (i) Mr. K. D. C. Vernon, F.L.A.
                      (ii) Mr. R. G. Griffin, F.L.A.
                      (iii) Mr. A. C. Townsend, M.A.
                      (iv) Mr. W. Pearson, B.Sc. (Econ.), A.L.A.
    (e) (Fine Arts—excluding Music)
    Subject Assessor :   Miss L. V. Paulin, M.A., F.L.A.
    Senior Examiner :   Mr. C. W. Musgrave, O.B.E., F.L.A.
    (f) (Music)
    Subject Assessor :   Dr. C. B. Oldman, C.V.O., C.B.,
                                      M.A., F.S.A., F.L.A.

    Senior Examiner :   Mr. R. L. W. Collison, F.L.A.

(*g*) (Medicine)
Subject Assessor :   Chairman of Board of Assessors.
Senior Examiner :   Mr. L. T. Morton, F.L.A.

(*h*) (History and Archaeology)
Subject Assessor :   Professor R. Irwin, M.A., F.L.A.
Senior Examiner :   Mr. T. S. Broadhurst, M.A., F.L.A.

(*i*) (General and European Philology).
Subject Assessor :   Miss L. V. Paulin, M.A., F.L.A.
Senior Examiner :   Mr. J. Bird, M.A., F.L.A.

1950 FINAL PART 4

(*a*) (Palaeography and Archives)
Subject Assessor :   Chairman of Board of Assessors.
Senior Examiner :   Mr. G. F. Osborn, F.L.A.

(*b*) (Library Work with Young People)
Subject Assessor :   Miss D. D. Chilcot, F.L.A.
Senior Examiner :   Miss B. M. L. Brazier, F.L.A.

(*c*) (1st Paper) (Advanced Classification)
Subject Assessor :   Mr. S. J. Butcher, F.L.A.
Senior Examiner :   Mr. E. R. J. Hawkins, F.L.A.
Senior Assistant Examiner :   Mr. C. A. Part, F.L.A.

(*c*) (2nd Paper) (Advanced Cataloguing)
Subject Assessor :   Mr. S. J. Butcher, F.L.A.
Senior Examiner :   Mr. E. F. Ferry, F.L.A.

(*d*) (Historical Bibliography)
Subject Assessor :   Professor R. Irwin, M.A., F.L.A.
Senior Examiner :   Mr. R. J. Roberts, M.A., A.L.A.
Senior Assistant Examiner :   Mr. K. G. Hunt, B.A., F.L.A.

(*e*) (Presentation and dissemination of information)
Subject Assessor :   Mr. D. V. Arnold, B.Sc., F.L.A.
Senior Examiner :   Mr. W. Ashworth, B.Sc., A.R.P.S.,
                                                        F.L.A.

(*f*) (Literature of Wales)
Subject Assessor :   Chairman of Board of Assessors.
Senior Examiner :   Mr. A. ap Gwynn, M.A.

ESSAYS
Assessor :   Chairman of Board of Assessors.

All correspondence relating to the examinations must be addressed to the Secretary and not to individual examiners.

APPROVAL OF LIBRARY SERVICE

Before a member may be registered as a Chartered Librarian he must, in addition to passing the necessary examinations, have completed a period of service in a library, and that service must be approved by the Library Association.

The Association will approve library service for this purpose only if one of the following conditions is satisfied in relation to the assistant who is a candidate for registration :

1. The assistant's professional training is under the constant supervision of a Chartered Librarian ;

or 2. The assistant will be brought regularly to a central point for practical instruction by a Chartered Librarian ;

or 3. The assistant will visit or be visited regularly by a Chartered Librarian for practical instruction.

Where the candidate for registration is serving in a library where there is no Chartered Librarian, it is the responsibility of the governing body of the library to find a Chartered Librarian in the neighbourhood who will accept the duty of supervising the professional training of the student.

Forms of application for approval may be obtained from the Secretary. If a certificate of approval is issued by the Association it will not have retrospective effect, and service undertaken before the date of approval cannot be reckoned by students as approved service.

Approval is not given to a library once and for all : service in a library ceases to be approved when it ceases to comply with the conditions of approval.

FELLOWSHIP THESIS

Associates of the Library Association of at least five years' standing will be elected as Fellows if they successfully complete a Thesis upon some aspect of librarianship. The Thesis is not part of the examination system. It is expected to be a demonstration of maturity in librarianship, and to be acceptable must be a worth-while contribution to professional knowledge.

Prospective fellows are permitted to propose their own subjects, and their attention is directed to a pamphlet entitled *Fellowship thesis* (price 1s. cash with order, from the Publications Officer, The Library Association, Chaucer House, Malet Place, London, W.C.1.) which gives full details regarding the choice and submission of subject, and the presentation of the Thesis.

The Board of Advanced Studies is responsible for the supervision of the Thesis arrangements. The Board currently consists of the following Fellows :

Mr. W. Ashworth, B.Sc., A.R.P.S. (*Chairman*).
Mr. S. J. Butcher.
Mr. D. J. Foskett, M.A.
Professor R. Irwin, M.A.

FACILITIES FOR STUDY AND TRAINING FOR THE EXAMINATIONS

1. Schools of Librarianship (with a note on financial assistance to students)
2. Sandwich Courses
3. Correspondence Courses
4. Part-time Courses
5. Summer Schools and Occasional Courses
6. Library Facilities

Schools of Librarianship

SPECIAL NOTE BY THE HON. SECRETARY OF THE ASSOCIATION OF BRITISH LIBRARY SCHOOLS

Applications for admission to full-time schools of librarianship

The attention of students is drawn to the following points :

1. The methods and procedures used in selecting full-time students differ from one school of librarianship to another. The known practice at one school should therefore not be treated as a guide to the practice at another school.

2. Students are not normally selected on the principle of " first come, first served", but on the basis of their suitability for full-time professional education. As applications must be accumulated and then assessed as a group before the selection is made, there is inevitably delay between application for admission and acceptance or rejection.

3. Students are advised to apply early, because the number of applications normally exceeds the number of places available.

4. An overseas student should have spent a period of practical experience in a library (preferably in his own country), be recommended by his Chief Librarian, be sponsored and financed by his government or by an international body and be educationally qualified to undertake a course.

LONDON.

SCHOOL OF LIBRARIANSHIP AND ARCHIVES, UNIVERSITY OF LONDON.

The University offers a Diploma in Librarianship, and a Diploma in Archive Administration.

LIBRARIANSHIP.

The course is open to graduates of approved universities, and applicants are normally expected to have obtained a year's experience of practical work in a library. Full-time students complete Part I of the course in one year, and continue with Part II (which consists of a bibliography or thesis) after leaving the School and obtaining a library post. Twelve months' full-time service in an approved library is required before the Diploma is awarded. The course for Part I includes the following subjects :

> History of Classical Libraries
> Background of English Libraries, Medieval and Modern
> Cataloguing and Classification
> Bibliography : materials and research in general and special fields

Elements of Historical Bibliography

One of the following :

(*a*) National and University Libraries
(*b*) Special Libraries
(*c*) Urban, County and School Libraries

One of the following :

(*a*) Palaeography and Diplomatic of English Archives
(*b*) Oriental and African Bibliography
(*c*) History and Literature of Science
(*d*) Advanced Historical Bibliography *and* Modern Book Production

ARCHIVES.

The course is open to graduates with a first or second class Honours degree in Arts. The course covers not less than one year, and includes the following subjects :

Palaeography and Diplomatic of English Archives
Administrative History
Archive Administration
Medieval Latin
Anglo-Norman French
History and Theory of Librarianship
National and University *or* Special Library Administration
or Public Library Administration
or Printed Materials and Sources for the Study of Archives.

Occasional students are accepted for any of the courses. Twelve months' full-time service in a record office approved for the purpose is required before the Diploma is awarded.

The Diploma courses include two or three weeks' practical work at libraries or record offices for all full-time students.

FEES.

The sessional composition fee for full-time students is £62 for a one-year course. Further particulars may be obtained from the Director, School of Librarianship and Archives, University College London, Gower Street, W.C.1.

SCHOOL OF LIBRARIANSHIP, NORTH WESTERN POLYTECHNIC.

The School offers full-time courses in preparation for the Part I and Part II Examinations of the Library Association. A number of short special courses will be offered in the session 1965-6 of which details will be published in the professional press.

Applications for places in the School of Librarianship will be accepted from those already working in libraries as well as from undergraduates and grammar school pupils while still at university or school. All students must on enrolment be over the age of 18 and have passed or been exempted from the Library Association's Entrance Examination.

For *non-graduates* the course will last two years and will cover the Part I and Part II Examinations of the Library Association. There will be no separate courses for either the Part I or Part II Examinations. *Graduates* exempted from the Part I Examination will prepare for the Part II Examination in a one-year course. Courses will be offered for *all* papers in the Part II examination syllabus, subject to sufficient demand. The course will begin in *January, 1966, but students entering on graduating or completing G.C.E. Advanced Level papers in the Summer of 1965, will enrol in September, 1965, and carry out a term's practical work in designated libraries.* This term's work is an integral and obligatory part of the course and will be supervised by the teaching staff of the school and by the staff of libraries with whom the School has made arrangements to accept students for this essential preliminary short training. This practical work follows a short induction course at the School. On completion of this practical work, students will join other students for formal studies in January, 1966.

In addition to this preparatory work *all* students will work in designated libraries not only to enrich their studies in the School, but to enable them to decide in which branches of librarianship their interests and aptitudes lie. Study tours of libraries in the United Kingdom and on the Continent also form an integral part of the course.

Overseas students intending to sit the Part I and Part II Examinations will be required to spend up to an additional year in the School's course for overseas librarians. This will enable overseas students to gain practical experience of librarianship in the U.K. and of the life and culture of the country as well as to study those aspects of librarianship of importance in their own countries but which are not part of the Library Association Syllabus. Overseas librarians with satisfactory educational qualifications not intending to sit these Examinations will also be considered for this course if they receive bursaries from their Government or from a recognized body such as Unesco or the British Council. No overseas student will be accepted without the approval of his Government's education authority or other appropriate body, *and overseas applicants for places in the School should take simultaneous steps to obtain this approval.*

Overseas graduate librarians preparing to sit the Part II Examination will be required to enrol for a period of up to two years and are advised to enquire of the Library Association at the earliest possible moment if their degree gives exemption from the Part I Examination.

Applications from overseas will not normally be considered from those who have not completed a satisfactory period of work as a full-time librarian.

Prospective students from the U.K. will be required to attend the School for interview.

All enquiries, other than those on matters of membership of the Library Association or eligibility for the examinations which should be addressed to the Association, should be made to the Head of the School of Librarianship, North-Western Polytechnic, Prince of Wales Road, London, N.W.5. (Phone : GULliver 1154, Ext. 24.) Application forms will be issued after October 1st, 1965 for courses beginning in September, 1966 and January, 1967.

Fees : £36 a year and £1 Students' Union Membership.

STAFF.

Head of School :   E. P. Dudley, F.L.A.
Senior Lecturers :   F. J. Bungay, F.L.A.
                      L. M. Harrod, F.L.A.
                      D. W. Langridge, B.A., Dip.Ed., A.L.A.
                      J. Mills, F.L.A. *(on secondment to*
                              Aslib Cranfield Research Project)
                      P. G. New, B.A., F.L.A.
Lecturers :   S. J. Brett, F.L.A.
                      J. Burkett, F.L.A.
                      Miss P. M. Fransella, F.L.A.
                      Mrs. L. M. Harrison, B.A.
                      T. S. Morgan, F.L.A.
                      J. Morris, M.A., F.L.A.
                      Miss B. M. Mulcahy, B.A., F.L.A.
                      C. D. Needham, F.L.A.
                      P. W. Plumb, F.L.A.
                      B. L. Redfern, F.L.A.
                      Mrs. D. M. Simpkins, B.Sc.
                      H. E. Taylor, F.L.A.
                      P. K. J. Wright, F.L.A.
Assistant Lecturers :   Miss M. J. Lewis, A.L.A.
                      Mrs. S. Simsova, F.L.A.
                      Miss E. N. von Schweinitz, A.L.A.
                      Mrs. P. J. Layzell Ward, F.L.A.

Three further teaching posts and a Research Assistantship are vacant.
A number of visiting lecturers participate in the work of the School.

SCHOOL OF LIBRARIANSHIP, EALING TECHNICAL COLLEGE.

This school provides a two-year full-time course for the examination syllabus of the Library Association. The syllabus consists of two examinations named the Part I and Part II Examinations respectively. Students are required to have complied with the regulations of the Library Association for admission to the Part I Examination.

A one-year course for graduates is also provided.

The course includes lectures, seminars and tutorials complemented by visits to libraries and other relevant institutions such as printing works, etc. Particular attention is paid to the needs of special librarians and this area of greater London is very fortunate in having many different special libraries in fairly close proximity which can be visited by students.

There is an excellent collection of books, pamphlets, periodicals, etc., relating to librarianship in the college library.

Applications for particulars and brochures should be made to the Principal, Ealing Technical College, St. Mary's Road, Ealing, W.5.

Fees : £25 10s. 6d. per annum or £8 13s. 6d. per term in-county.
        Out-county on application.
        Students' Union fee of £1 1s. 0d.

STAFF.

Director :	E. F. Browning, F.L.A.
Staff :	A. Blum, Ph.D.
	D. Cashmore, B.Sc., B.Mus., F.R.C.O., A.R.C.M., L.R.A.M.
	S. J. Green, F.L.A.
	L. C. Guy, F.L.A.
	E. W. B. Jones, M.A., A.L.A.
	Miss A. Powell, Ph.D.
	Mrs. S. Sayed, F.L.A.
	S. Sidders, *Lecturer in bookbinding.*
	E. R. Stone, F.L.A.
	A. R. Thomas, F.L.A.
	Miss W. Todd, B.A., F.L.A.
	J. R. Tooley, B.A., A.L.A.
Tutor-Librarian :	A. J. Dickson, B.A., F.L.A.

Visiting lecturers also assist in teaching specialist subjects.

PROVINCES.

SCHOOL OF LIBRARIANSHIP, CITY OF BIRMINGHAM COLLEGE OF COMMERCE.

This School provides full-time courses for the Part I and Part II Examinations, including a wide range of choice in the optional subjects.

A Prospectus giving further particulars of these courses may be obtained from the Principal, City of Birmingham College of Commerce, Gosta Green, Birmingham 4.

Course fee *per annum* £50.

STAFF.

Principal Lecturer :	R. Northwood Lock, F.L.A.
Senior Lecturer :	Graham Jones, M.A., F.L.A.
Lecturers :	E. S. Fox, F.L.A.
	F. Hughes, F.L.A.
	K. Davison, F.L.A.
	D. W. Hope, B.A., F.L.A.
	A. Croghan, A.L.A.
	R. Hewitt, A.L.A.
	C. Ray, F.L.A.

A panel of Visiting Lecturers operates regularly in tuition for special subjects.

SCHOOL OF LIBRARIANSHIP, BRIGHTON TECHNICAL COLLEGE.

Commencing in September of each year the School provides a two-year full-time course for non-graduates wishing to prepare for the Part I and Part II examinations of the Library Association. The course is an integrated one, and, though students will sit for the Part I examination at the end of their first year, enrolments will be made only for the complete two-year course. A balanced selection of papers from the Part II examination syllabus is offered, catering for a variety of professional and subject interests.

Included in the course are lectures, seminars and tutorials. Opportunities are provided for students to inspect reference materials, etc., in a number of libraries in Brighton and its neighbourhood, and practical instruction in bookbinding is given in cooperation with the Brighton College of Art and Crafts. Class visits are made to libraries of various types, and to other establishments of professional interest, in London and elsewhere. Part of the course consists of a period of practical work under instruction (not less than four weeks) in a designated library; a number of libraries in different parts of the country cooperate in making this instruction possible. It normally takes place in July at the end of the first year.

A prospectus giving further particulars may be obtained, together with a form of application, from The Registrar, Brighton Technical College, Richmond Terrace, Brighton 7. Completed applications should be returned to him by February 28th prior to the commencement of the course.

Before final acceptance applicants must possess the following qualifications:

Either (*a*)   a General Certificate of Education with passes in at least five subjects, one of which must be English Language, and not less than two of which must be at Advanced level:

Or, as a temporary measure (*b*) a Pass in the First Professional Examination or Entrance Examination of the Library Association, or a certificate of exemption from either of those examinations.

Applications will be considered from persons sitting for Advanced level subjects in the General Certificate of Education examination held in the Summer prior to the commencement of the course, but enrolment cannot be completed until examination results are known.

Students without previous experience of library work will be required to spend a short period in a suitable library before the course begins.

STAFF.

W. H. C. Lockwood, M.A., F.L.A.
C. Bradley, M.A., A.L.A.
B. Hunnisett, F.L.A.
A. J. Simpson, F.L.A.

SCHOOL OF LIBRARIANSHIP, LEEDS COLLEGE OF COMMERCE.

The courses for non-graduate candidates will begin in September each year and will run for seven terms. The fourth of those terms will be spent by all non-graduate students in libraries which offer courses of practical instruction as a supervised part of the essential requirements of the College. The courses for graduate candidates will normally run for three terms.

The minimum alternative qualifications for entry to courses for non-graduate candidates are (1) two ' A ' level G.C.E. subjects with acceptable gradings. Preference will be given to candidates who offer a science at ' A ' level, or two sciences at ' O ' level. (2) the First Professional Examination or the Entrance Examination of the Library Association together with at least five ' O ' level G.C.E. subjects. Only acceptable marks or gradings in either of the examinations will be considered as qualifications.

Both non-graduate and graduate students will be required to submit written examples of previous work, the standard of which will be taken into account as a further qualification for entry to courses.

All courses will include a considerable programme of privately prepared projects which are subjected to tutorial criticism. Non-graduate students will also be required to carry out a number of extensive projects in the summer vacations of each of the two complete years of their courses. The projects are an essential part of the courses and will be taken into account when assessments are made of the students' examination and sessional work.

The courses aim at a wide professional education and they are also intended to test and develop students' capacity to apply an advanced technology in specialized branches of librarianship, and to develop their ability to show initiative when faced with professional responsibility.

Besides the term of practical instruction already noted students are expected to make a number of visits to libraries and other organizations and in the second year to take part in an organized residential tour of certain London libraries.

The demands made on students will be not less than those made by university courses. Candidates will therefore need to take responsibility for reaching the appropriate standard.

The personal fees are £50 for each session of three terms, and the balance of costs is met by payment from the national pool for advanced courses.

A prospectus is available from the Head of the School, Leeds College of Commerce, 43 Woodhouse Lane, Leeds 2.

STAFF

Head of the School :	Neville E. Dain, F.L.A.
Lecturers :	T. Brimelow, F.L.A.
	D. E. Davinson, F.L.A.
	G. Jefferson, F.L.A.
	L. Corina, B.A.
	P. A. Gaskill, M.A.
	J. Hart, M.A.
	J. F. Myers, M.A., LL.B.
Lecturer in Printing :	D. J. Juniper
Visiting Lecturers :	Dr. R. T. Bottle, B.Sc., F.R.I.C.
	C. A. Crossley, F.L.A.
	H. Nichols, F.L.A.
	E. G. Twigg, F.L.A.

SCHOOL OF LIBRARIANSHIP, CITY OF LIVERPOOL COLLEGE OF COMMERCE.

The School provides Sandwich, Full-time, and Post-Graduate Courses in Librarianship for the Part I and Part II Examinations. Courses begin each January and July.

The Sandwich course for non-graduates extends over a period of three years, the student completing the in-College period and normally his examinations at the end of two-and-a-half-years. The College year is divided into four ten-week terms. Students commencing in January are in-College during the first two terms of the year and those commencing in July are in-College in the third and fourth terms. Students may be library-based or College-based but the latter should preferably have had a year's experience in a library.

During the out-of-College period students normally return to their own libraries ; arrangements between students for exchange of libraries during these times are encouraged.

Graduates and suitable non-graduates who have passed the Part I Examination can be integrated into Sandwich Courses for the Part II Examination.

During the out-of-College period, contact is maintained by correspondence, a newsletter and visits by tutors. Students are set projects and written work during this period.

Because of the flexible nature of the end-on Sandwich method, it is possible for students to attend full-time for two years to complete the course. Graduates with suitable practical experience can likewise attend for a one year post-graduate course.

Certain Libraries on Merseyside are prepared to offer temporary paid posts to recommended Sandwich Course students and most libraries have offered unpaid training facilities to students during the out-of-College period.

Further particulars and application forms from the Lecturer-in-charge, School of Librarianship, College of Commerce, Tithebarn Street, Liverpool 2.

Fees: Full-time (Sandwich 3 years) £36 p.a.
   ,,   ,, (Two year continuous) £50 p.a.

STAFF

Senior Lecturer in charge :	W. H. Snape, D.P.A., F.L.A.
Lecturers :	R. G. Astbury, F.L.A.
	A. Maltby, B.A., F.L.A.
	One vacancy
Visiting Lecturers :	E. T. Bryant, F.L.A.
	N. Carrick, B.A., F.L.A.
	M. Devereux, F.L.A.
	A. C. O. Ellis, F.L.A.
	B. Houghton, A.L.A.
	J. G. McPeake, F.L.A.
	Miss S. M. Pinches, A.L.A.
	P. D. Pocklington, F.L.A.
	Mrs. I. D. Sell, B.A.
	A. C. Symons, B.A., F.L.A.

SCHOOL OF LIBRARIANSHIP, LOUGHBOROUGH COLLEGE OF FURTHER EDUCATION.

The School of Librarianship is primarily concerned with two main groups of students. Students with the necessary two ' A ' level General Certificate of Education subjects, as required by the Association's regulations, can apply to be admitted to the two-year course. This is an integrated programme designed to take a student through the Part I and Part II examinations of the Library Association in successive years. A one-year course is also provided for graduates for the Part II examination. All communications regarding enrolment for these courses should be addressed to the School of Librarianship, Loughborough College of Further Education, Loughborough, Leicestershire. A brochure, giving an outline of the courses and the facilities provided, can be obtained on request.

STAFF

Head of Department :	Roy Stokes, M.A., D.L.C.(Hon.), F.L.A.
Senior Lecturer :	P. J. Cox, F.L.A.
Lecturers :	K. Anderson, F.L.A.
	A. C. Foskett, F.L.A.
	H. Nichols, F.L.A.
	J. G. Ollé, F.L.A.
	J. McC. Orr, F.L.A.
	Miss F. P. Parrott, F.L.A.
	Miss B. Ramsbotham, F.L.A.

SCHOOL OF LIBRARIANSHIP, MANCHESTER COLLEGE OF COMMERCE.

The Department of Librarianship offers full-time courses in preparation for the Part I and Part II Examinations of the Library Association: (i) for *University graduates*, a course of four terms, commencing in September and leading to the Part II Examination in December of the following year; (ii) for *Non-graduates*, a two-year course commencing in January and leading to the Part I Examination in December of the first year, and the Part II Examination in December of the second year.

The courses comprise lectures, seminars and tutorials, supplemented by visits to libraries and book production establishments, special lectures given by senior practising librarians, prescribed practical work in libraries and study tours.

Tuition fees are as follows:

University graduates: £65 for the course.

Non-graduates: £50 for each year of the course.

All applications from *overseas* students must be sponsored by an official body or chief librarian in the country concerned, or by the British Council, and overseas applications which do not comply with this requirement will not be considered. Graduates of universities overseas are advised to apply to the Library Association at an early stage, for exemption from the Part I Examination, because applications for admission to the postgraduate course cannot be considered if such exemption is not granted.

Applications for admission to the School should be sent to the Head of Department, School of Librarianship, Manchester College of Commerce, 103 Princess Street, Manchester 1, from whom full particulars of the courses may be obtained.

STAFF.

Head of the Department :   Philip M. Whiteman, F.L.A.
Senior Lecturer :   J. L. Ingham, F.L.A.
Lecturers :   R. H. Bartle, B.Litt., M.A., F.L.A.
  J. D. Lee, F.L.A.
  D. B. Lomas, A.L.A.
  Miss M. R. Roberts, F.L.A.
  A. G. Shaw, B.A., F.L.A.
  A. H. Thompson, F.L.A.
  K. A. Whittaker, F.L.A.
  A. J. Wood, F.L.A.

Additional full-time lecturers are being appointed. The full-time staff is assisted by a team of Visiting Lecturers.

DEPARTMENT OF LIBRARIANSHIP, NEWCASTLE MUNICIPAL COLLEGE OF COMMERCE.

The Department provides a two-year full-time course for non-graduates who have been working in libraries for the Part I and Part II Examinations of the Library Association ; a seven-term course for holders of the G.C.E. with at least two A.L. subjects who enter direct from the sixth form for the same examinations ; and a four-term course for graduates in preparation for the Part II examination.

The courses consist of a programme of lectures, tutorials, seminars, practical work and visits to libraries and book trade firms. Lectures are also given by specialist librarians and technical experts where appropriate.

Full details are set out in the prospectus of the Department, which may be obtained on application to the Head of the Department of Librarianship, Municipal College of Commerce, College Street, Newcastle upon Tyne, 1.

STAFF.

Head of Department :   W. Caldwell, F.L.A.
Lecturers :   Miss M. Johnson, M.A., F.L.A.
  Miss J. Knott, B.A., F.L.A.
  J. Stephenson, F.L.A.
  W. M. Watson, F.L.A.
  T. D. Wilson, F.L.A.
Assistant Lecturers :   J. Allread, F.L.A.
  Miss A. D. Noble, F.L.A.
  Two appointments pending.

POSTGRADUATE SCHOOL OF LIBRARIANSHIP, UNIVERSITY OF SHEFFIELD.

The Diploma

The Postgraduate School of Librarianship offers a full-time course of one academic year leading to the University of Sheffield's Diploma in Librarianship. The Library Association recognizes the Diploma as qualifying its holders for exemption from the examinations leading to the Associateship of the Library Association and the Department of Scientific and Industrial Research has recognized the course in Scientific and Industrial Librarianship as suitable for the tenure of its Advanced Course Studentships.

Entrance qualifications

Preference will normally be given to candidates with first- or second-class honours degrees who have had a year of practical experience in a library or information service before joining the course. Considerable emphasis will be placed on work with materials in foreign languages and an adequate reading knowledge of two languages other than English is a condition of entry.

The Syllabus

This may be considered as made up of two groups of subjects. The first and smaller group is taken by all students and provides the background essential for effective work in libraries and information services of all types.

The subjects which make up the second, and main, group are chosen in accordance with a student's specialized requirements. Some are suitable for graduates in all disciplines who wish to prepare for academic or public librarianship, others for graduates in science and technology who wish to study scientific and industrial librarianship and information work.

1. *Academic and Public Librarianship*

By a systematic study of the literature and bibliography of a special field—the humanities or the social sciences or the pure and applied sciences—students will direct their specialized subject knowledge to the needs of librarianship. They will also follow a course on historical bibliography which will trace the main developments in book production from the earliest times to the present day. The basic course in cataloguing and classification, followed by all students, will in the case of this group be supplemented by an advanced course on the linguistic, technical and administrative aspects of this work. Finally, this group will follow a course in either public or academic librarianship, in which they will study the relevant history, the functions, aims and general organization of libraries in the chosen field, with special emphasis on significant new trends and the likely needs of libraries in the future.

2. *Scientific and Industrial Librarianship and Information Work*

This course is intended for graduates in science and technology and has been recognized by the Department of Scientific and Industrial Research as suitable for the tenure of its Advanced Course Studentships.

Students following this course will study the organization and administration of scientific and industrial libraries and information services. They will make an intensive survey of the literature and bibliography of science and technology and in a course on Scientific and Technical Documentation will study the means by which information is organized, stored, retrieved, reproduced and transmitted. Account will be taken of the specialized problems of cataloguing and classification associated with scientific information work; theory and practice of indexing (conventional and non-conventional) and abstracting; manual and machine literature searching; editorial work and the preparation of reviews of literature; foreign language material and its associated problems.

Fees

Composition fee (covers registration, union membership, tuition and examinations, but not re-examination or the cost of visits and field course). £70

Applications for entrance to the School

Application forms may be obtained from The Registrar, The University of Sheffield, Western Bank, Sheffield, 10. Applications should be made by December 31st for the course starting the following October. Candidates to whom places are offered can expect to be informed by early April.

NORTHERN IRELAND.

SCHOOL OF LIBRARIANSHIP, QUEEN'S UNIVERSITY, BELFAST.

For particulars of the Diploma to be offered by Queen's University, Belfast, application should be made to the Clerk of Admissions, Queen's University, Belfast, 7, N. Ireland.

SCOTLAND.

SCHOOL OF LIBRARIANSHIP, THE UNIVERSITY OF STRATHCLYDE (SCOTTISH COLLEGE OF COMMERCE).

The School provides a two-year full-time course extending from October to June for one session in preparation for the Part I and Part II Examinations of the Library Association. The fee is £50. Methods of tuition include lectures, demonstrations, discussion, visits to printing, binding and similar establishments, and periods of practical training in representative libraries.

The syllabus of the School and forms of application for courses may be had from the University of Strathclyde (Scottish College of Commerce), Pitt Street, Glasgow, C.2.

STAFF.

Head of School :	W. E. Tyler, F.L.A.
Lecturers :	W. R. Aitken, M.A., Ph.D., F.L.A.
	L. L. Ardern, F.L.A.
	F. McAdams, F.L.A.
	C. Smith, F.L.A.
	Miss G. Louise M. Snodgrass, M.A., F.L.A.
	J. A. Tait, M.A., F.L.A.
	R. S. Walker, F.L.A.
	H. A. Whatley, F.L.A.

Lecturers in English :	D. H. McAllister, M.A., B.Litt.
	Miss J. McInnes, M.A.
	J. Redmond, M.A., Ed.B.
Lecturer in Geography :	Miss J. C. K. McKinlay, B.Com., Dipl. Com.
Lecturer in History :	Thomas McAloon, M.A.
Part-time Lecturers :	Miss E. Beswick, M.A.
	Miss D. White, M.A., A.L.A.

WALES

COLLEGE OF LIBRARIANSHIP, WALES

This is the first independent College in the United Kingdom to specialize in the study of Library Science. Newly established in 1964 the College offers full-time courses in preparation for Part I and Part II Examinations of the Library Association.

Courses are provided for graduates, direct entrants from schools and entrants with library experience. The College has close links with the National Library of Wales, University, Public and Special libraries. For all courses practical experience and knowledge is recognized as a necessary supplement and complement to theoretical study. To provide and to enlarge such experience, study tours of libraries in the United Kingdom and overseas and conurbation studies will be arranged and regarded as an integral part of the course.

Post Graduate Course

The graduate course consists of four terms from October to December of the following year. The work of the first term is of an introductory nature and is regarded as a necessary preliminary to the Part II course commencing in January. A feature of the first term's work will be the emphasis placed upon practical work in chosen libraries.

Non-Graduate Courses

(i) Direct entrants from school and other entrants without appropriate library experience holding G.C.E. qualifications with two or more subjects taken at Advanced Level undertake a seven-term course beginning in October leading to the Part II Examination in December two years later. The work of the first term is regarded as an introduction to the more formal studies of Part I. During this period an attempt will be made to provide students with a practical and theoretical framework that will make easier the transition to Part I studies.

(ii) Entrants with appropriate library experience possessing the requisite qualifications recognized by the Library Association will attend for a six-term course beginning in January leading to the Part II Examination in December of the following year.

Overseas Students

Overseas students may apply for places in the College providing they have the necessary qualifications and the financial backing of their Government or of another recognized body such as the British Council or Unesco.

Overseas students should write to the Library Association on matters of membership or eligibility to take the examinations. Graduates should write to the Library Association to obtain exemption from the Part I examination. Copies of certificates of exemption should be enclosed with applications.

Fees

Post graduate course (four terms)	£72 os. od.
Two-year course for students with appropriate library experience (six terms)	£108 os. od.
Two years and one-term course for students without appropriate library experience (seven terms)	£126 os. od.

Students of the College of Librarianship, Wales, will be full members of the Students' Union of the University College of Wales, Aberystwyth.

Residential Accommodation

Residential accommodation will be provided from 1965.

STAFF

Principal :	F. N. Hogg, D.P.A., F.L.A.
Senior Lecturers :	C. D. Batty, B.A., F.L.A.
	D. J. Grogan, B.A., F.L.A.
	N. Roberts, B.A., F.L.A.
	R. E. Sturt, F.L.A.
Lecturers :	*Six additional staff will be appointed in 1965.*

Visiting Lecturers

Senior Librarians from National, University, Public and Special libraries will take a full part in the courses.

Application forms and copies of the prospectus may be obtained from : The Principal, College of Librarianship, Bronpadarn, Llanbadarn Fawr, Aberystwyth.   Tel. No. Aberystwyth 7286.

OVERSEAS.

SCHOOL OF LIBRARIANSHIP, GHANA.

The School offers a full-time two-year course leading to the Part I and Part II Examinations.

In the near future courses will relate specifically to African circumstances and will include practical training in suitable libraries.

A limited number of places are offered to students outside Ghana.

Further information can be obtained from the Principal, Ghana Library School, P.O. Box 2362, Accra, Ghana.

STAFF.

Principal :	R. C. Benge, M.C., F.L.A.
Lecturers :	John Roe, F.L.A.
	John A. Villars, A.L.A.
	John E. Linford, F.L.A.
Visiting Lecturer in French Language :	F. K. Adinyira, B.A.

INSTITUTE OF LIBRARIANSHIP, UNIVERSITY OF IBADAN, NIGERIA.

Courses leading to an Ibadan Diploma in Librarianship are open to graduates and to others with two years' full-time library experience and part of the Registration Examination. Tuition is in English.

Fees : Board and residence £90 per session
Tuition £90 per session
payable at the beginning of each session.

Enquiries should be addressed to the Director, Institute of Librarianship, University of Ibadan, Nigeria.

STAFF.

Director : W. J. Harris, B.A.(Oxon.), F.N.Z.L.A.

Lecturer in Bibliography : J. Packman, B.A.(Lond.), Dip. Lib.(Lond.), F.L.A.

Lecturer in Cataloguing and Classification : A. Nitecki, M.A.(Chicago).

Lecturer in Reference Sources and Assistance to Readers : F. Adetowun Ogunsheye, M.A.(Cantab.) M.L.S. (Simmons).

Lecturer in Administration : *Not yet filled.*

FINANCIAL ASSISTANCE TO STUDENTS.

Local Education Authority awards are available to students from all kinds of libraries (University, Special and Public). Application should be made to the Education Officer for the area in which the student resides.

Students employed by local authorities may be eligible for assistance under the National Joint Council *Scheme of conditions of service, and amendments* : (section 8, Post-entry Training—Financial Assistance).

Some library authorities have their own schemes of training which include payment for attendance at Library school. It is advisable to enquire about this from prospective employers.

Mitchell Memorial Fund.—This Fund, which is maintained by subscriptions from members, is applied to the provision of loans for members wishing to attend a whole-time School of Librarianship. Applications for a loan should be addressed to the Secretary, The Library Association, Chaucer House, Malet Place, London, W.C.1.

The amount of the fund at present available is small, but it is confidently believed that members will continue to subscribe to it with the object of assisting an increasing number of students.

Correspondence Courses

Courses for the Entrance Examination and for the 1950 Final Examination are offered under the auspices of the Association of Assistant Librarians. Sessions are arranged twice yearly : a spring session running from April to June of the following year, and an autumn session running from November to December of the following year. The closing date for the spring session is 28th February and for the autumn session 30th September.

Courses are also available in Papers 103, 106, 402 and 504 of List C in Part II of the 1964 Syllabus. These courses are intended for Associates requiring an additional paper and for transitional students nearing completion of studies under the new Syllabus. Sessions will be run annually, commencing April and finishing June of the following year. Completed applications to be submitted by 28th February.

Revision courses are also arranged for Old Finals students, running March-June and September-December each year. Closing date for these are 20th February and 25th August, respectively. Full details of subjects offered and their fees are available from the A.A.L. Honorary Education Officer, Mr. J. S. Davey, 49 Halstead Gardens, London, N.21. All applications and enquiries should be accompanied by a stamped addressed envelope.

NOTE. The A.A.L. do not offer courses for the 1964 Part I and Part II Examination syllabuses.

The final session for the Entrance Examination course will run from November 1965 to November 1966. The last sitting for the Entrance Examination will be Winter 1967.

Part-time Courses

Classes for the Library Association Examinations have been held in the past at the following institutions. Particulars of courses to be offered in the future may be obtained from the Principal, unless otherwise stated.

LONDON AREA.

CATFORD College of Commerce, Plassy Road, Rushy Green, S.E.6. HITher Green 4843.

CLAPHAM JUNCTION College of Commerce, Plough Road, St. John's Hill, S.W.11. BATtersea 2600.

CROYDON Technical College, Fairfield, Croydon. CROydon 9271/5.

EALING Technical College, St. Mary's Road, W.5. EALing 0162/3.

HARROW Technical College. For particulars apply to Kenton Branch Library, Kenton Lane, Kenton, Middlesex.

KINGSTON College of Further Education, Kingston Hall Road, Kingston-upon-Thames, Surrey. KINgston 0880. (Entrance only.)

KINGSTON College of Technology, Penrhyn Road, Kingston-upon-Thames, Surrey. KINgston 1127.

NORTH-WESTERN POLYTECHNIC, Prince of Wales Road, N.W.5. GULliver 1154/5. For further particulars apply to the Head of the Department of Librarianship.

WANDSWORTH Technical College, High Street, Wandsworth, S.W.18.

WEST HAM College of Further Education, North Street, Plaistow, E.13. GRAngewood 1259.

WEST LONDON College of Commerce, Airlie Gardens, Campden Hill Road, W.8. PARk 4550.

PROVINCES.

BIRMINGHAM College of Commerce, Aston Street, Birmingham 4. MIDland 6267/9.

BLACKPOOL Technical College, Palatine Road, Blackpool. Blackpool 29071-6.

BRADFORD Technical College, Great Horton Road, Bradford 7. Bradford 28837.

BRIGHTON Technical College, Brighton 7. Brighton 26544.

BRISTOL College of Commerce, Unity Street, Bristol 1. Bristol 2-3016.

COVENTRY Technical College, Butts, Coventry. Coventry 25032.

DERBY and District College of Technology, Business Studies and Management Department, Kedleston Road, Derby. Derby 47181. For further particulars apply to the Head of the Department.

DONCASTER Technical College, Waterdale. Doncaster 4495.

FARNBOROUGH Technical College, Boundary Road, Farnborough, Hants. Farnborough 1940/1.

GLOUCESTER Technical College, Brunswick Road. Gloucester 21191.

HUDDERSFIELD College of Technology, Huddersfield, Yorks. Huddersfield 30501.

ISLE OF WIGHT Technical College, Hunnyhill, Newport, Isle of Wight. Newport 3511/2.

KINGSTON UPON HULL College of Commerce, Brunswick Avenue, Kingston upon Hull. Kingston upon Hull 26333.

LEEDS College of Commerce, 43 Woodhouse Lane, Leeds 2. (Entrance Examination and transitional courses only.)

LEICESTER Colleges of Art and Technology, The Newarke. Leicester 50181.

LINCOLN Technical College, Cathedral Street. Lincoln 24416.

LIVERPOOL College of Commerce, 79 Tithebarn Street, Liverpool, 2. MARitime 1781.

MEDWAY College of Technology, Horsted, Maidstone Road, Chatham. Chatham 41001-2-3.

MIDDLESBROUGH. Constantine College of Technology, Middlesbrough. Middlesbrough 44176.

NEWPORT and MON. College of Technology, Allt-yr-yn Avenue, Newport, Mon. Newport 66936.

NORTHAMPTON College of Technology, St. George's Avenue, Northampton. Northampton 34286-7.

NOTTINGHAM. Clarendon College of Further Education, Pelham Avenue, Nottingham. Nottingham 62201-3.

OXFORD College of Technology, Headington Road, Oxford. Oxford 63434.

READING Technical College, King's Road, Reading, Berks. Reading 54451.

ST. ALBANS College of Further Education, St. Albans, Herts.

SHEFFIELD College of Technology, Pond Street, Sheffield, 1. Sheffield 29671.

SHREWSBURY Technical College, London Road, Shrewsbury. Shrewsbury 51544.

SLOUGH College, William Street, Slough. Slough 27511.

SOUTHAMPTON College of Technology, East Park Terrace, Southampton. Southampton 29381.

STOCKTON-BILLINGHAM Technical College, Roseberry Road, Billingham. Stockton 52101.

STOKE-ON-TRENT College of Commerce, Stoke Road, Shelton, Stoke-on-Trent. Stoke-on-Trent 22256-7.

TROWBRIDGE and West Wilts College of Further Education, College Road, Trowbridge. Trowbridge 4081.

SCOTLAND.

ABERDEEN Commercial College, St. Clement Street, Aberdeen. Aberdeen 52528/9.

GLASGOW. Scottish College of Commerce, Pitt Street, Glasgow, C.2. Central 6901.

WALES.

COLWYN BAY. The Technical College, Stuart Drive, Rhos-on-Sea, Colwyn Bay. Colwyn Bay 44980.

Summer Schools and Occasional Courses

SCHOOL LIBRARIES

A course on School Libraries will be organized in 1965 by the British Council. It will be held from June 21st-July 2nd. Applications should be made to the nearest office of the British Council, or to the Director, Courses Department, The British Council, 65 Davies Street, London, W.1.

LONDON.

In the Autumn of each year the Greater London Division of the Association of Assistant Librarians holds a week-end school on some topical aspect of librarianship. The next is to be held at Glenwood Hotel, Cliftonville from October 29th-31st, 1965. Revision schools for the Examinations have been discontinued for the present owing to lack of demand. All enquiries should be addressed to the Hon. Secretary, Miss J. Nicholson F.L.A., Church End Library, 9 Hendon Lane, London, N.3.

SCOTLAND.

A Summer School of Librarianship, under the auspices of the Scottish Library Association will be held at Newbattle Abbey College, seven miles from Edinburgh, from July 3rd-9th, 1965.

All enquiries should be addressed to the Honorary Secretary, Scottish Library Association Summer School, Mr. J. W. Cockburn, F.L.A., Depute City Librarian, Central Library, George IV Bridge, Edinburgh 1.

YOUTH LIBRARIES GROUP.

The Week-End School will be held in 1965 at St. Salvator's Hall, St. Andrews University, from September 3rd-5th. Further details from the Honorary Secretary.

THE LIBRARY OF THE ASSOCIATION.

A library of books, periodicals, pamphlets and other documents on libraries and library technique is maintained by the Library Association at Chaucer House (see map). The Library incorporates part of the students' library of text-books formerly administered by the Association of Assistant Librarians and the Library of the North Midlands Branch of the Library Association, and also includes a valuable collection of plans, photographs, slides and other illustrations of libraries of all kinds, British and foreign.

The aim is to make the collection the most comprehensive library of librarianship in the world and to that end every effort is made to acquire all appropriate books and periodicals published abroad as well as material published in Great Britain. The library receives currently over four hundred and fifty British and foreign periodicals in the fields of library Science, Bibliography and allied subjects, and annual reports and bulletins from many libraries and library organizations all over the world.

Over 30,000 volumes and pamphlets as well as about 800 runs of periodicals are held in stock and approved Essays submitted as part of the Examinations under earlier syllabuses as well as Theses submitted under the 1964 Fellowship regulations are deposited in the Library and may be freely consulted. All the material in the Library is open to access by members.

The Library may be used for reference purposes and as a lending library for home study and, therefore, contains duplicate copies of a considerable number of books, periodicals and photographs, particularly those items which are needed for the Library Association Examinations. Care is taken to stock sufficient copies to meet the demand, although allowance is made for the fact that most text-books for students of librarianship will be available in the candidate's own library. All relevant new material is purchased as published and occasional translations are commissioned of important foreign articles or pamphlets. A printed catalogue of the Library was published in 1958. A photocopying service is available.

The Library is on the third floor of Chaucer House, where a spacious and attractive reading room is provided with seats for twenty-four readers. Here are displayed, on open shelves, a large proportion of the stock and a good selection of the periodicals currently taken. All members of the Association are invited to make the fullest possible use of the library facilities which include postal loans and are given with a minimum of formalities. The Rules will be found below and attention is drawn to the fact that except for two months in the summer the Library is open on Tuesday and Thursday evenings until 8 p.m.

The Library is also an Information Department and a great amount of material has been acquired in order to deal with requests for information about all aspects of librarianship historical and current except for those such as education, membership, staffing and grading which are dealt with by other departments of the Library Association. These requests are received from individuals, library authorities and other organizations in all parts of the world, and members are invited to make use of the service provided by writing, telephoning or calling personally. All librarians and library assistants can help in the work by sending to the Library Association notes of interesting developments and experiments in librarianship, information about new buildings and new methods of administration, annual reports of libraries and library organizations, bulletins, booklists and other appropriate literature. All will be warmly welcomed.

The Council for Microphotography and Document Reproduction is currently administered from the Library and a collection of material on microphotography and document reproduction is being built up. Various microtext readers are available for demonstration purposes in the Library.

Rules.

1. The Library is available for all members of the Association.

2. The Library is open, for reference and lending purposes, from 9 a.m. to 6 p.m. on Mondays, Wednesdays and Fridays, from 9 a.m. to 8 p.m. on Tuesdays and Thursdays (except during the period mid-July to mid-September when the closing time will be 6 p.m.) and 9 a.m. to 12 noon on Saturdays. The Library is not open on Public Holidays.

3. Books may be borrowed by members of the Association for a period of *ten weeks*, except certain books in constant demand which are issued for *one month*. This period may be extended if the books are not required by another member. Members must make an application for renewal.

4. Four books, excluding periodicals, may be borrowed at one time. In special circumstances this number may be increased at the discretion of the Librarian.

5. When a book is sent by post (other than by air mail) the borrower is required to pay the cost of returning the book only. Where a book is sent by air mail the borrower is required to pay postage both ways. The lending of rare or valuable books is at the discretion of the Librarian.

6. Books must be securely packed for return to the Library.

7. Borrowers will be held fully responsible for the safe custody and return of books borrowed by them.

8. It shall be within the discretion of the Librarian to refuse the use of the Library to any member persistently disregarding the Rules.

9. Communications respecting the use of the Library should be addressed to The Librarian, The Library Association, Chaucer House, Malet Place, London, W.C.1. and should not be embodied in letters on other subjects addressed to the Secretary.

OTHER LIBRARIES.

The Greenwood Library for Librarians, a department of The Manchester Public Libraries, is a collection of works on bibliography, library economy and history, bookbinding, and the history of printing, publishing and bookselling.

The Library is intended primarily for the use of professional librarians and students of librarianship. Many books may be borrowed for home reading from the Central Lending Library, St. Peter's Square, Manchester 2, by personal callers who present current readers' tickets of any library authorities, or through the normal machinery of inter-library lending.

The original collection of Thomas Greenwood, presented to The Manchester Public Libraries by him in 1904, contained approximately 10,000 books and pamphlets. His will provided a legacy of £5,000, the proceeds of which have been devoted to the extension of the collection, and the Library has also been augmented by additions bought by The Manchester Public Libraries, and by donations from many libraries and individuals.

The *Bermondsey Central Library,* under the Metropolitan Special Collections scheme, holds over 7,500 volumes and pamphlets and 95 files of periodicals on librarianship and bibliography. Requests for loans should be addressed to the Chief Librarian, Bermondsey Central Library, Spa Road, London, S.E.16.

PUBLICATIONS OF
THE LIBRARY ASSOCIATION

(Prices to members are given within brackets. All prices are post free. Orders from individuals not exceeding £2 must be accompanied by remittance. Postage and packing on overseas parcels will be charged separately.)

BOOKS FOR YOUNG PEOPLE: Eleven to thirteen plus.   3rd edition, 1960.   239 p. 16s. 8d. (12s. 6d.)
Fourteen to seventeen.   85 p.   1957.   6s. 8d. (4s. 6d.)

BURKETT (J.) and MORGAN (T. S.), *editors*.   Special materials in the library. 1963.   (reprinted, 1964.)   177 p.   40s. (30s.)

CATALOGUING RULES: AUTHOR AND TITLE ENTRIES.   1908 edition, reprinted. 1964.   xx, 88 p.   13s. 8d. (10s.)

CLARKE (I. F.)   The tale of the future from the beginning to the present time. 1961.   165 p.   Illus.   20s. (15s.)

COATES (E. J.)   Subject catalogues: headings and structure.   1960   (reprinted). 186 p.   22s. 8d. (17s.)

CORBETT (E. V.)   Public library finance and accountancy.   1960 (reprinted). xi, 212 p.   24s. 8d. (18s. 6d.)

CROUCH (M. S.)   Books about children's literature.   1963.   31 p.   6s. (4s. 6d.)

CROUCH (M. S.)   Treasure seekers and borrowers.   1962 (reprinted).   160 p. Illus.   30s. (22s. 6d.)

CUTTER (C. A.)   Rules for a dictionary catalog.   4th edition, reprinted.   1962. 173 p.   13s. 8d. (10s.)

EAGER (A. R.)   Guide to Irish bibliographical material.   1964.   xiii, 392 p. £4 16s. (£3 12s.)

FOSKETT (D. J.) and PALMER (B. I.), *editors*.   The Sayers Memorial Volume: essays in librarianship in memory of William Charles Berwick Sayers. 1961.   218 p. portrait.   36s. (27s.)

GOING (Mona E.), *editor*.   Hospital libraries and work with the disabled.   1963. 186 p.   Illus.   44s. (33s.)

HOGG (F. N.), MATTHEWS (W. J.) and VERITY (T. E. A.)   A report on a survey made of book charging systems at present in use in England.   1961. 192 p.   18s. 8d. (14s.)

IRWIN (R.) and STAVELEY (R.) The libraries of London.   2nd rev. edition, 1961 (reprinted, 1964.) 332 p.   40s. (30s.)

JOLLIFFE (H.) Public library extension activities. 1962. 344 p. Illus. 68s. (51s.)

LIBRARY ASSOCIATION.   Catalogue of the Library.   1958.   vii, 519 p.   £6 7s.

THE LIBRARY IN THE HOSPITAL AND CARE IN THE COMMUNITY.   Papers given at a Conference, July 1963.   1964.   32 p.   9s. (6s. 9d.)

LINE (M. B.)   A bibliography of Russian literature in English translation to 1900 (excluding periodicals).   1963.   74 p.   24s. (18s.)

MEDICAL SECTION.   Directory of medical libraries in the British Isles.   2nd edition, 1965.   viii, 108 p.   36s. (27s.)

MUNBY (A. N. L.)   The libraries of English men of letters.   (Esdaile Memorial Lecture.)   1965.   19 p.   3s. 6d.

MUNFORD (W. A.)   Edward Edwards, 1812-1886: portrait of a librarian. 1963.   240p.   Illus.   48s. (36s.)

NATIONAL LIBRARIES: Extracts from the proceedings of the University and Research Section Conference, Bangor.   1963.   56p.   10s. (7s. 6d.)

PALMER (B. I.)   Itself an education : six lectures on classification.   1962. 72 p.   16s. (12s.)

PROFESSIONAL AND NON-PROFESSIONAL DUTIES IN LIBRARIES.   1962.   77 p. 18s. (13s. 6d.)

PUBLIC LIBRARY BUILDINGS :   THE WAY AHEAD.   1960.   12 p.   Illus.   1s.

RANGANATHAN (S. R.)   Prolegomena to library classification.   2nd edition. 1957.   487 p.   45s. 8d. (33s. 6d.)

ROBERTS (C.)   Buried books in antiquity.   (Esdaile Memorial Lecture.)   1963. 16 p.   3s. 6d.

ROBINSON (M. W.)   Fictitious beasts: a bibliography.   1961.   76 p.   14 illus. 14s. 8d. (11s.)

SOME PROBLEMS OF A GENERAL CLASSIFICATION SCHEME.   Report of a Conference, June 1963.   1964.   47 p.   10s. (7s. 6d.)

STUDENTS' HANDBOOK.   Annual.   3s.

THORNTON (J. L.) and TULLY (R. I. J.)   Scientific books, libraries and collectors. Second, revised edition.   1962.   xiii, 406 p.   Illus.   68s. (51s.)

THORNTON (J. L.) *and others.*   A select bibliography of medical biography. 1961.   112 p.   Illus.   27s. 6d.   (20s. 6d.)

THWAITE (M. F.)   From primer to pleasure: an introduction to the history of children's books from the invention of printing to 1900.   1963.   318 p. Illus.   68s. (51s.)

TOASE (Mary), *editor.*   Guide to current British periodicals.   1962.   ix, 256 p. 70s. (52s. 6d.)

WALFORD (A. J.) *editor.*   Guide to foreign language grammars and dictionaries. 1964.   132 p.   30s. (22s. 6d.)

WALFORD (A. J.), *editor.*   Guide to reference material supplement.   1963. 370 p.   £4 (£3)

YEAR BOOK, 1965.   14s. (10s. 6d.)

PERIODICALS

LIBRARY ASSOCIATION RECORD.   Monthly.   £5 5s. p.a.   (Free to members.)

LIBRARY SCIENCE ABSTRACTS.   Quarterly.   Edited by H. A. Whatley.   50s. (35s.) per annum.   Cumulative index to vol. 7-11, 1956-1960.   40s. 8d. (30s. 6d.)

SPECIAL SUBJECT LISTS.   General editor: Harold Smith.

BRITISH HUMANITIES INDEX.   Quarterly with annual cumulation.   Edited by Peter Ferriday.   £10 4s. (£8 8s.) for 3 quarterly issues and annual cumulation.   £8 8s. (£7) for annual cumulation only.

BRITISH TECHNOLOGY INDEX. Monthly with annual cumulation. Edited by
E. J. Coates. £15 15s. per annum. £9 9s. for annual cumulation only.
BRITISH EDUCATION INDEX. Compiled by the English Institutes of Education.
Six termly parts and bi-annual cumulation, £5.

L.A. PAMPHLETS

The following are available:

No. 8. Children's periodicals of the XIXth century. (S. A. Egoff.) 1951.
55 p. 5s. 4d. (3s. 9d.)

No. 13. English county maps. (R. J. Lee.) 1955. 32 p. 3s. 4d. (2s. 3d.)

No. 18. Archives and manuscripts in libraries. (P. Hepworth.) 2nd ed.
1964. 69 p. Illus. 12s. (9s.)

No. 19. The Anglo-American Library Associations. (R. D. Macleod.) 1958.
13 p. 2s. 4d. (1s. 9d.)

No. 20. The reproduction of catalogue cards. (P. S. Pargeter.) 1960 (reprinted).
48 p. 9s. (6s. 9d.)

No. 21. University extra-mural libraries. (E. P. Pritchard.) 1961. 5s. 4d.
(3s. 9d.)

No. 22. A Soviet view of British libraries. (V. I. Shunkov, C. G. Firsov and
N. I. Tyulina.) 1961. 30 p. 5s. 4d. (3s. 9d.)

No. 23. The hospital library in Sweden. Translated from the Swedish. 1962.
40 p. Illus. 10s. (7s. 6d.)

READERS' GUIDES

Obtainable from E. H. Roberts, F.L.A., Hon. Publications Officer, County
Libraries Group (Lindsey & Holland County Library, 45 Newland, Lincoln),
to whom all enquiries should be addressed, or from Library Association Head-
quarters.

Copies of the following guides are still available:

No. 61. Agriculture. 3rd ed. 1961. 6d.
No. 64. Keeping Pets. 1961. 6d.
No. 68. Mountaineering. 1962. 1s.
No. 71. Antiques. 1963. 2s. 6d.
No. 72. Handicrafts. 2nd ed. 1963. 2s. 6d.
No. 73. Natural History. 1963. 2s. 6d.
No. 74. Choice of Careers. 5th ed. 1964. 2s. 6d.
No. 75. Electrical Engineering. 2nd ed. 1964. 2s. 6d.
No. 76. The Face of Scotland. 2nd ed. 1964. 2s. 6d.
No. 77. Sailing, Cruising and Motorboating (June) 1964. 2s. 6d.
No. 78. Sources of Local History. (July) 1964. 2s. 6d.
No. 79. Fishing and Angling. (Aug.) 1964. 2s. 6d.
No. 80. Mathematics. (Sept.) 1964. 2s. 6d.
No. 81. Children's Books. (Oct.) 1964. 2s. 6d.
No. 82. Medieval Britain. (Nov.) 1964. 2s. 6d.

The price for individual copies is 2s. 6d. There is a reduced price for
copies in excess of five, of which particulars may be obtained from the Publications Officer.

Guides to the following subjects are in preparation—Mexico and South
America; Reluctant reader (2nd ed.); Jazz (2nd ed.); Economics; Victorian
Britain; Stagecraft and the Theatre; Stuart and Tudor Britain.

A.A.L. PUBLICATIONS

Obtainable from J. S. Davey, F.L.A., 49 Halstead Gardens, London, N.21, to whom all enquiries should be addressed.

BENGE (R. C.) Bibliography and the provision of books. 1963. 30s. (20s.)

BINNS (N. E.) An introduction to historical bibliography. 2nd ed. 1962. 40s. (30s.)

CALDWELL (W.) Introduction to county library practice. 2nd ed. 1964. 12s. (8s.)

CLOUGH (E. A.) Bookbinding for librarians. 1957. 30s. (20s.)

CORBETT (E. V.) The public library and its control. 1962. 18s. (12s.)

COTTON (G. B.) and GLENCROSS (A.) Cumulated fiction index, 1945-1960. 1961. 80s. (60s.)

ENSER (A. G. S.) Filmed books and plays; 4th supplement. 1963. 15s. (10s.)

HOLLIDAY (S. C.) The reader and the bookish manner. Illus. by G. W. Harris. 1953. 3s. 9d. (2s. 9d.)

JOHNSON (A. F.) Practical cataloguing. 2nd ed. 1963. 15s. (10s.)

PHILLIPS (W. H.) A primer of book classification. 5th ed. 1962. 18s. 6d. (12s. 6d.)

SAYERS (W. C. B.) First steps in annotation. 1955. 2s. 9d. (2s. 3d.)

The Reprint Series:

    CRANSHAW (J.) Cutting catalogue costs to 50 per cent. 10d. (8d.)

    JENKINS (R.) Paper-making in England, 1495-1788. 4s. (3s.)

A.A.L. Guides to Professional Examinations:

    The Final Examination:

        Part 1. Bibliography and book selection. 2nd ed. 1959. 8s. 6d. (7s.)

        Part 2. Library organization and administration: with 2c. Special libraries and information bureaux. 2nd ed. 1961. 8s. 6d. (7s.)

        Part 4c. Advanced classification and cataloguing. 1956. 4s. 9d. (3s. 9d.)

Periodical:

    THE ASSISTANT LIBRARIAN. Monthly. 15s. per annum. (Free to members.) (Back numbers 1s. 3d.)

LONDON & HOME COUNTIES BRANCH PUBLICATIONS

Obtainable from T. D. F. Barnard, A.L.A. East Sussex County Library, Southdown House, St. Anne's Crescent, Lewes, Sussex, to whom all enquiries should be addressed.

Notes for tutors: First Professional Examination. 1959. 2s. 6d.

Notes for tutors: Registration, classification and cataloguing. 1960. 2s. 6d.

Notes for tutors: The study of reference material. 3rd rev. ed. 1962. 3s. 6d.

Library education today. 1958. 2s. 6d.

London Union List of Periodicals. 2nd edition. 1958. £1.

Handlist of bibliographies on exhibition at the Library Association Conference, Hastings, 1954. 1s.

Report on the library system of London and the Home Counties, 1959.   1961.
   13s. 6d.

Branch Conference papers:

1961: The changing pattern of librarianship.   6s.

1962: Book provision for special needs.   5s.

1963: Looking both ways.   8s. 6d.

1964: Librarianship overseas.   8s. 6d.

REFERENCE, SPECIAL AND INFORMATION SECTION

   The following publications of the Section and its regional Groups are now
available, and may be purchased from the Association's offices at Chaucer
House, Malet Place, London, W.C.1. Postage, either Inland or Foreign, is not
included in the prices quoted, except where indicated.

Reference Library Staffs, edited by F. H. Fenton, F.L.A. London, the Section,
   15s. (11s. 6d.) post free.   1962.   68 p.

Reference Library Stocks, edited by F. H. Fenton., F.L.A. London, the Section,
   6s. (5s.).   1960.   48 p.

Basic Stock for the Reference Library, edited by A. J. Walford, M.A., Ph.D.,
   F.L.A., and Charles A. Toase, A.L.A. London, the Section, 1s. post free.
   1964.   24 p.

Catalogue of Miniature and Full Orchestral Scores in Yorkshire Libraries,
   compiled by K. G. E. Harris, Leeds, Yorkshire Group, 25s.   1960.   200 p.

Directory of Yorkshire Library Resources. Leeds, Yorkshire Group, 15s.   1961.

Library Resources in the West Midlands, 2nd ed., edited by B. G. Staples.
   Birmingham, West Midlands Group, 28s. (21s.).   1963.   88 p.

The Libraries of Greater Manchester, compiled by Harold Smith. Manchester,
   North Western Group, 15s.   1956.   92 p.

Union List of Periodicals in Northern Libraries, compiled by the Northern
   Group. London, the Section, 20s. (15s.) post free.   1963.

Newspapers First Published before 1900 in Lancashire, Cheshire and the Isle
   of Man: a Union List of Holdings in Libraries and Newspaper Offices in
   that Area, edited by R. E. G. Smith, F.L.A., North Western Group.
   London, the Section, 13s. (10s. 6d. to Members) post free.   1954.   47 p.

Union List of Current Abstracting, Indexing and Review Serials in the North
   and East Midlands, edited by A. C. Foskett, F.L.A., North Midlands
   Group. London, the Section, 6s. (5s. to Members) post free.   1964.   42 p.

Annual Conference Papers

Current Problems, 1956 (1956 Conference proceedings), edited by Harold Smith,
   F.L.A. and Norman Horrocks, F.L.A. London, the Section, 3s. (2s. 6d.).
   1956.   44 p.

Technical Problems of Reference and Special Libraries (1957 Conference proceedings), edited by Harold Smith, F.L.A., and H. G. German, F.L.A. London, the Section, 3s. (2s. 6d.). 1957. 48 p.

Information Services, National and International (1958 Conference proceedings), edited by Harold Smith, F.L.A. London, the Section, 3s. (2s. 6d.). 1958. 42 p.

Proceedings of the 7th Annual Conference, edited by O. James. London, the Section, 6s. (5s.). 1960. 52 p.

The Library and the Research Worker (Proceedings of the Joint Annual Conference, 1960), edited by J. Munro, London, the Section, 6s. (5s.). 1961. 40 p.

The Two Cultures (1961 Conference proceedings), edited by Joan M. Harvey, A.L.A. London, the Section, 6s. 6d. (5s. 6d.), post free. 1962.

Looking Ahead (1963 Conference proceedings), edited by K. J. Rider, F.L.A. London, the Section, 10s. (7s. 6d. to Members) post free. 1963. 38 p.

Inservice Training (1964 Conference proceedings). 1964. 47 p. 10s. (7s. 6d. to members) post free.

Aids to Reference Service Series

1. The County of London: a select book list, by the senior staff of the Guildhall Library. London, South Eastern Group, 4s. 6d. (3s. 6d.). 1959. 32 p.

Library Resources in the Greater London Area Series

2. Photographic literature: a symposium. London, South Eastern Group, 2s. 9d. (2s.). 1953. 20 p.

5. Agricultural libraries. London, South Eastern Group, 4s. 6d. (3s. 6d.). 1956. 20 p.

6. Zoological libraries, compiled by A. C. Townsend and G. B. Stratton. London, South Eastern Group, 4s. 6d. (3s. 6d.). 1957. 21 pp.

Occasional Papers of the North Western Group

1. Library Classification and the Field of Knowledge, by D. J. Foskett. Manchester, North Western Group, 2s. 6d. 1958. 15 p.

2. John Benjamin Dancer, . . . originator of micro-photography, by L. L. Ardern. Manchester, North Western Group, 4s. ($0.75 in U.S.A. and Canada). 1960. 16 p.

3. The Creed of a Librarian—No Politics, no Religion, no Morals—, by D. J. Foskett. Manchester, North Western Group, 3s. 6d. 1962. 13 p.

EASTERN BRANCH PUBLICATION

Obtainable from Miss A. Parry, Central Public Library Norwich, NOR 57E.

East Anglian bibliography. Quarterly. £2 2s. p.a. 1960—(back issues 10s. 6d. each).

YEAR BOOK, 1965

List of members

The membership addressing system of the Association is in the process of being changed from Addressall to Addressograph and, with it, the method of producing the List of Members which normally appears in the *Year Book*. Under the new system, the List of Members will be produced by photo-litho from lists run off from the Addressograph plates. Before printing, every member will be sent a copy of his entry and asked to check that it is correct. This will result in a more accurate and up-to-date list than was possible under the previous system.

The change in the system is a lengthy one and the List of Members was not ready for production in time to be included in the 1965 *Year Book*.

The *Year Book*, 1966, which will include the List of Members in its new style, will be ready by March, 1966.